The message of hope

Compiled by
Yusuf Jamal

The Message of Hope

yusuf jamal

Published by yusuf jamal, 2023.

While every precaution has been taken in the preparation of this book, the publisher assumes no responsibility for errors or omissions, or for damages resulting from the use of the information contained herein.

THE MESSAGE OF HOPE

First edition. June 29, 2023.

ISBN: 979-8223394150

Written by yusuf jamal.

Dedicated to all knowledge seekers of the world

In the name of GOD, the Most Gracious, the Most Merciful

Dedication

To the name of GOD, the Almighty, the Most Gracious, the Most Merciful, the Creator, the Sustainer, the Beneficent, the Benevolent, the Infinite, the Lord of all the creations. All praise is to GOD and peace and prayers are upon all his prophets and Messengers.

Disclaimer

This book is only a selection of verses from holy Quran and not the whole Quran. All of these verses have been selected from the point of view of hope, positive thinking and good tidings as the core of Quran. The introduction and translation used here is by maulana Waheeduddin Khan. No original work or proprietorship is claimed. It is aimed to spread positivity all around. This work can, partially or wholly and without any change in original text and context, be cited or shared or distributed in print or any digital forms without the permission or knowledge of the author. For translation to any other language refer to authentic source.

About the author

Prof. Yusuf Jamal

Post Graduate Department of Physiology-Unani

Ayurvedic & Unani Tibbia College, New Delhi, India

Email- yousufjamal289@gmail.com

Table of contents

18.85. The Day will surely come when We shall gather the God-fearing like [honored] guests before the Compassionate God.

Prologue

Divine Verses: The Message of Hope is a collection of some of the most powerful and inspiring verses from the Holy Quran. The Quran, the sacred book of Islam, contains guidance and wisdom that has touched the hearts and minds of millions of people around the world for over fourteen centuries.

In this book, we have brought together a selection of verses that speak to the fundamental message of hope that is at the heart of the Quran. These verses offer comfort and guidance in times of adversity, and remind us of the goodness, compassion and mercy of Allah (SWT) and his creation plan.

In today's world, where we are facing unprecedented challenges, from pandemics to personal, social and political upheaval, it is more important than ever to seek guidance and hope from sources that inspire and uplift us. The Quran provides a source of light and guidance for those who seek it, and these divine verses offer a message of hope that can provide comfort and solace in even the darkest of times.

As you read through this collection, you will be inspired by the words of Allah (SWT) and find comfort in the knowledge that a mighty force is always with you, helping you and guiding you towards the path of righteousness and salvation. May this book serve as a reminder of the power of hope and the transformative effect it can have on our lives.

May Allah (SWT) bless us all and guide us towards the straight path.

Amen.

Yusuf Jamal

Introduction

From Quran translation by maulana Waheeduddin Khan

The Quran is a book of God revealed to the Prophet Muhammad. It did not come to him in the form of a complete book, but in parts over a period of 23 years. The first part was revealed in 610 AD, when the Prophet Muhammad was in Makkah. Subsequently, different parts continued to be revealed regularly, the final part being revealed in 632, when the Prophet was in Madinah. There are 114 chapters in the Quran, both long and short. The verses number about 6600. To meet the needs of recitation, the Quran was divided into 30 parts. These parts were finally set in order under the guidance of the Angel Gabriel, through whom God had revealed the Quran.

The Quran is the Book of God. It has been preserved in its entirety for all time to come. Although written originally in Arabic, it has been made accessible, thanks to translations, to those who have no knowledge of Arabic. While no substitute for the original, translations serve the signal purpose of spreading the word of God far beyond the Arabic-speaking peoples to a far broader spectrum of humanity.

The Quran is apparently in the Arabic language, but in reality, it is in the language of nature, that is, the language in which God directly addressed all human beings at the time of Creation. This divine invocation of humanity is ever-present in the consciousness of all human beings that is why the Quran is universally understandable—to some on a conscious plane and to others at the subconscious level. This reality has been described in the Quran as 'clear revelations in the hearts of those who have been given knowledge.' This verse goes on to say that 'none deny our revelations save the wrongdoers' (29:49).

This means that the Divine Reality, explained by the Quran on a conscious plane, pre-exists in man at the level of the subconscious. The message of the Quran is not, therefore, something which is alien to man. It is in fact a verbal expression of that same Divine Reality which is in consonance with man's own nature and with which he is already familiar. The Quran explains this by saying that those born in later times were all initially born at the time of the creation of Adam and, at that time, God had directly addressed all these human souls.

This event is thus alluded to in the Quran:

[Prophet], when your Lord brought forth the offspring from the loins of the Children of Adam and made them bear witness about themselves, He said, 'Am I not your Lord?' and they replied, 'Yes, we bear witness that You are.' So you cannot say on the Day of Resurrection, 'We were not aware of this' (7:172).

In the following verse, the Quran makes further mention of the dialogue between God and man: 'Surely We offered Our trust to the heavens and the earth, and the hills, but they shrank from bearing it and were afraid of it. And man undertook it. But he has proved a tyrant and a fool' (33:72). The Quran, for man, is in essence already known to him, rather than an entirely unknown entity. In reality, the Quran is the unfolding of the human mind.

When one whose nature is alive—having saved himself from later conditioning—reads the Quran, those brain cells will be activated wherein God's first address lies preserved. If we keep this in mind, it will not be difficult to appreciate that the translation of the Quran is a valid means of understanding it.

If God's address was the First Covenant, the Quran is the Second Covenant. Each testifies to the veracity of the other. If one has little or even no grasp of the Arabic language, and can read the scriptures only in translation, he should not anticipate that he will be frustrated in his understanding of the Quran, for the Quranic concept of human as the natural recipient of God's word has become a reality in modern times. The science of the genetic code and the findings of anthropology both fully support this viewpoint.

The Creation Plan of God

Every book has its objective and the objective of the Quran is to make human aware of the Creation plan of God. That is, to tell humanity why God created this world; what the purpose is of settling human on earth; what is required from human in his pre-death life span, and what he or she is going to confront after death.

Human is born as an eternal creature. When God created man as such, He divided his life span into two periods, the pre-death period, which is a time of trial, and the post-death period, which is the time for receiving the rewards or punishment merited by one's actions during one's lifetime. These take the form of eternal paradise or eternal hell.

The purpose of the Quran is to make human aware of this reality. This is the theme of this divine Book, which serves to guide man through his entire journey through life into the after-life.

It would be correct to say that human is a seeker by birth. These questions lurk in everyone's mind: Who am I? What is the purpose of my life? What is the reality of life and death? What is the secret of man's success and failure? Etc.

According to the Quran, the answer to these questions is that the present world is the testing ground and whatever man has been endowed with in his pre-death period is all a part of the test. The Hereafter is the place where the result of the test will be taken into account by the Almighty and whatever man receives in the life after death, by way of reward or punishment, will be commensurate with his deeds in this world.

The secret of a human's success in this life is to understand God's creation plan and map out his/her life accordingly.

A Book of Divine Warning

The Quran is a book of divine warning. A combination of lessons and admonitions, it would be even more appropriately called a book of wisdom. The Quran does not follow the pattern of the traditional didactic book. In fact, when the average reader picks up the Quran, it appears to him to be a collection of fragmentary statements. Apparently this feeling is not unreal. But this arrangement of the Quran is not due to any shortcoming, but is rather in conformance with the Quranic plan of retaining its original form in order to fulfill its purpose of conveying the message of truth to the reader who may, in his forays into the scriptures, read only one page, one verse or one line at a time.

One vital aspect of the Quran is that it is a reminder of the blessings granted by the Supreme Benefactor. The most important of these are the exceptional qualities with which God endowed man when He created him. Another great blessing is that He settled him on the earth, a planet where all kinds of support systems existed for his benefit. The purpose of the Quran is to ensure that, while enjoying these blessings of nature, man will keep his Benefactor in mind: he must acknowledge the munificence of his Creator. It is in so doing that man will gain entry into eternal paradise; ignoring his Benefactor, on the other hand, will lead man straight to hell. The Quran is indeed a reminder of this inescapable reality.

The Inner Spirit and God Realization

One important quality of the Quran is that it gives us only basic, but essential principles, often resorting to reiteration to emphasize them. On the contrary, non-basics, or matters relating only to form, constitute only a negligible part of the scriptures. This is in consonance with the Quranic scheme, the importance of form being entirely secondary.

To the Quran, only those precepts are important which figure as fundamental guidelines. This aspect of the Quran is so clear that its reader cannot but appreciate it.

The truth is that the inner spirit is of the utmost importance in the building of the Islamic personality. Once the inner spirit is developed, correct form will naturally ensue. But form on its own can never produce the inner spirit. That is why the aim of the Quran is to initiate and bring to fruition an intellectual revolution within man. The expression used by the Quran for this intellectual revolution is *ma'rifah* (realization of truth) (5:83). The Quran stresses the importance of man's discovery of truth at the level of realization. True faith in God is what one achieves at such a level. Where there is no realization, there is no faith.

The Word of God

When you read the Quran, you will repeatedly find it stated that it is the word of God. Apparently this is a plain fact. But when seen in context, it is an extraordinary statement. There are many books in the world which are believed to be sacred. But, except for the Quran, we do not find any religious book which thus projects itself as the word of God. This kind of statement, appearing uniquely in the Quran, gives a point of departure to the reader. He then studies it as an exceptional book, rather than as a common book written by human beings. We find recurring in the Quran statements worded more or less as follows, 'O man, it is your Lord, who is addressing you. Listen to His words and follow Him.' Even this style of address is quite exceptional. This kind of direct divine invocation is not present in any other book. It leaves a lasting impression on man. He feels his Lord is directly addressing him. This feeling compels man to take the assertions of the Quran with extreme seriousness, rather than treat them like everyday statements in an ordinary book.

The style of compilation of the Quran is also unique. Books written by human beings usually have their material arranged in order from A to Z, according to the topic. But the Quran does not follow a pattern of this kind, so that to the common man it appears to be lacking in order. When looked at in reality, however, it will emerge as an extremely coherent and orderly book, and quite majestic in its style of writing. While reading the Quran, we feel that its writer is on a very high pedestal from where He is looking down and addressing the whole of humanity, which is His special concern. This address focuses on different groups of human beings, while encompassing all of them.

One special aspect of the Quran is that at any moment its reader can consult its Writer, put his questions and receive answers, for the Writer of the Quran is God Himself. He is a living God. As man's Creator, He directly hears and answers man's call.

Peaceful Ideological Struggle

Those who are introduced to the Quran only through the media, generally have the impression that the Quran is a book of *jihad*, and *jihad* to them is an attempt to achieve one's goal by means of violence. But this idea is based on a misunderstanding. Anyone who reads the Quran for himself will easily appreciate that its message has nothing to do with violence. The Quran is, from beginning to end, a book which promulgates peace and in no way countenances violence. It is true that *jihad* is one of the teachings of the Quran. But *jihad*, taken in its correct sense, is the name of peaceful struggle rather than of any kind of violent action. The Quranic concept of jihad is expressed in the following verse, 'Do greater *jihad* (i.e. strive more strenuously) with the help of this [Quran]' (25:52).

Obviously, the Quran is not a weapon, but a book which gives us an introduction to the divine ideology of peaceful struggle. The method of such a struggle, according to the Quran, is 'to speak to them a word to reach their very soul' (4:63).

So, the desired approach, according to the Quran, is one which moves man's heart and mind. That is, in addressing people's minds, it satisfies them, convinces them of the veracity of the Quran and, in short, brings about an intellectual revolution within them. This is the mission of the Quran. And this mission can be performed only by means of rational arguments. This target can never be achieved by means of violence or armed action. It is true that there are certain verses in the Quran, which convey injunctions similar to the following, 'Slay them wherever you find them' (2:191). Referring to such verses, there are some who attempt to give the impression that Islam is a religion of war and violence. This is totally untrue. Such verses relate, in a restricted sense, to those who have unilaterally attacked the Muslims. The above verse does not convey the general command of Islam.

The truth of the matter is that the Quran was not revealed in the complete form in which it exists today. It was revealed from time to time, according to the circumstances, over a time span of 23 years. If this is divided into years of war and peace, the period of peace amounts to 20 years, while that of state of war amounts only to 3 years. The revelations during these 20 peaceful years were the peaceful teachings of Islam as are conveyed in the verses regarding the realization of God, worship, morality, justice, etc. This division of commands into different categories is a natural one and is found in all religious books.

For instance, the Bhagwad Gita, the holy book of the Hindus, pertains to wisdom and moral values. Yet along with this is the exhortation of Krishna to Arjuna, encouraging him to fight (Bhagavad Gita, 3:30). This does not mean that believers in the Gita should wage wars all the time. Mahatma Gandhi, after all, derived his philosophy of non-violence from the same Gita. The exhortation to wage war in the Gita applies only to exceptional cases where circumstances leave no choice. But for general day-to-day existence it gives the same peaceful commands as derived from it by Mahatma Gandhi. Similarly, Jesus Christ said, 'Do not think that I came to bring peace on Earth. I did not come to bring peace, but a sword.' (Matthew, 10:34).

It would not be right to conclude that the religion preached by Christ was one of war and violence, for such utterances relate purely to particular occasions. So far as general life is concerned, Christ taught peaceful values, such as the building up of a good character, loving each other, helping the poor and needy, etc.

The same is true of the Quran. When the Prophet Muhammad emigrated from Makkah to Madinah, the idolatrous tribes were aggressive towards him. But the Prophet always averted their attacks by the exercise of patience and the strategy of avoidance. However on certain occasions no other options existed, save that of defense. Therefore, he had to do battle on certain occasions. It was these circumstances, which occasioned those revelations relating to war. These commands, being specific to certain circumstances, had no general application. They were not meant to be valid for all time to come. That is why; the permanent status of the Prophet has been termed a 'mercy for all mankind.' (21:107).

Islam is a religion of peace in the fullest sense of the word. The Quran calls its way 'the paths of peace' (5:16). It describes reconciliation as the best policy (4:128), and states that God abhors any disturbance of the peace (2:205). We can say that it is no exaggeration to say that Islam and violence are contradictory to each other.

Now starts your journey to God realization and self discovery.

Hope is here for you.

Read on.

Chapter wise selection

The opener (Al Fatiha)

1.1. All praise is due to God, the Lord of the Universe;

1.2. The Beneficent, the Merciful;

1.3. Lord of the Day of Judgment,

1.4. You alone we worship, and to You alone we turn for help,

1.5. Guide us to the straight path:

1.6. The path of those you have blessed; neither of those who have incurred your wrath, nor of those who have gone astray.

The Heifer (Al Baqra)

2.2. This is the Book; there is no doubt in it. It is a guide for those who are mindful of God,

2.3. who believe in the unseen, and are steadfast in prayer, and spend out of what We have provided them with;

2.4.those who believe in the revelation sent down to you and in what was sent before you, and firmly believe in the life to come

2.5. They are the people who are rightly following their Lord and it is they who shall be successful.

2.20. God has power over all things.

2.21. People, worship your Lord, who created you and those before you, so that you may become righteous,

2.22 who made the earth a bed, and the sky a canopy; and it is He who sends down rain from above for the growth of every kind of fruit for your sustenance.

2.37. He is the Forgiving One, the Merciful.

2.38. when guidance comes to you from Me, anyone who follows My guidance will have no fear, nor will they grieve.

2.45. Seek help with patience and prayer; this is indeed an exacting discipline, but not to the humble,

2.54. He is the Forgiving One, the Merciful.

2.58. We shall forgive you your sins and We shall give abundance to those who do good.'

2.62. The believers, the Jews, the Christians, and the Sabaeans— all those who believe in God and the Last Day and do good deeds—will be rewarded by their Lord; they shall have no fear, nor shall they grieve. 2.82. but those who believe and do good works are the heirs of Paradise; there they shall abide forever.

2.85. God is never unaware of what you do.

2.105. God is limitless in His great bounty.

2.106. Do you not know that God has power over all things?

2.107. Do you not know that the kingdom of the heavens and the earth belongs to God alone, and that there is no protector or helper for you besides God?

2.110. Any good you store up for yourselves, you will find it with God. Certainly, God sees what you do.

2.112. Indeed, those who submit themselves to God and act righteously shall be rewarded by their Lord: they shall have no fear, nor shall they grieve.

2.115. The East and the West belong to God. Whichever way you turn, there is the Face of God. God is all pervading and all knowing.

2.116. Everything in the heavens and the earth belongs to Him; all things are obedient to Him.

2.117. He is the Originator of the heavens and the earth, and when He decrees something, He says only, 'Be!' and it is.

2.127. Our Lord, accept this from us; for You are All Hearing, All Knowing.

2.128. Lord, make us submissive to You; make of our descendants a nation that will submit to You. Teach us our rites of worship and turn to us with mercy; You are the Forgiving One and the Merciful.

2.134. Those were a people that have passed away; what they did is theirs and what you have done is yours. You will not be answerable for their deeds.

2.136. It is to Him that we surrender ourselves.

2.138. We take on God's own dye. Who has a better dye than God's? We worship Him alone.

2.142. The East and the West belong to God. He guides whom He pleases to the right path.

2.143. God will never let your faith go to waste. God is compassionate and merciful to mankind.

2.147. Truth is what comes from your Lord; therefore, do not be of those who doubt.

2.152. So remember Me; I will remember you. Be thankful to Me and do not be ungrateful.

2.153. You who believe seek help through patience and prayer; surely, God is with the steadfast.

2.155. We shall certainly test you with fear and hunger, and loss of property, lives and crops. Give good news to those who endure with fortitude.

2.158. Of anyone who does good of his own accord, God is appreciative, and aware.

2.163. Your God is one God. There is no deity save Him. He is the Compassionate, the Merciful.

2.164. In the creation of the heavens and the earth; in the alternation of night and day; in the ships that sail the ocean bearing cargoes beneficial to man; in the water which God sends down from the sky and with which He revives the earth after its death, scattering over it all kinds of animals; in the courses of the winds, and in the clouds pressed into service between earth and sky, there are indeed signs for people who use their reason.

2.172. Believers, eat the wholesome things which We have provided for you and give thanks to God, if it is Him you worship.

2.173. For God is forgiving and merciful.

2.177.Virtue does not consist in whether you face towards the East or the West; virtue means believing in God, the Last Day, the angels, the Book and the prophets; the virtuous are those who, despite their love for it, give away their wealth to their relatives and to orphans and the very poor, and to travelers and those who ask [for charity], and to set slaves free, and who attend to their prayers and pay the alms, and who keep their pledges when they make them, and show patience in hardship and adversity, and in times of distress. Such are the true believers; and such are the God-fearing.

2.186. When My servants ask you about Me, say that I am near. I respond to the call of one who calls, whenever he calls to Me: let them, then, respond to Me, and believe in Me, so that they may be rightly guided.

2.190. God does not love aggressors.

2.195. Do good, God loves the doers of good.

2.197. Whatever good you may do, God is aware of it. Make provision for yourselves—but surely, the best of all provision is God consciousness. Always be mindful of Me, you that are endowed with understanding.198and remember Him as He has guided you. Before this you were surely astray.

2.209. Know that God is mighty and wise.

2.210. All things return to God.

2.213. God guides whom He will to a straight path.

2.214. Surely the help of God is near.

2.222. He loves those who keep themselves clean.

2.223. Give good tidings to the believers.

2.224. God is all hearing and all knowing.

2.231. and know that God is aware of everything.

2.233. and know that God is observant of all your actions.

2.234.God is aware of what you do.

2.247. God is magnanimous and all knowing.

2.249. God is indeed with the steadfast.

2.251.God is bountiful to humankind.

2.255. God: there is no deity save Him, the Living, the Eternal One. Neither slumber nor sleep overtakes Him. To Him belong whatsoever is in the heavens and whatsoever is on the earth. Who can intercede with Him except by His permission? He knows all that is before them and all that is behind them. They can grasp only that part of His knowledge which He wills. His throne extends over the heavens and the earth; and their upholding does not weary Him. He is the Sublime, the Almighty One!

2.256. There shall be no compulsion in religion:

2.257. God is the patron of the faithful. He leads them from darkness to the light.

2.258. God does not guide the wrongdoers.

2.260. God is infinite and all knowing.

2.263. A kind word and forgiveness is better than a charitable deed.

2.264. God is self sufficient and forbearing.

2.265. God sees what you do.

2.267 Believers, give charitably from the good things which you have earned and what We produce for you from the earth; not worthless things which you yourselves would only reluctantly accept.

2.268. God promises His forgiveness and His bounty.

2.269. whoever is granted wisdom has indeed been granted abundant wealth. Yet none bear this in mind except those endowed with understanding.

2.271. God is aware of all that you do.

2.279. Do not wrong [others] and you will not be wronged.

2.282. Be mindful of God; He teaches you: He has full knowledge of everything.

2.284. All that the heavens and the earth contain belongs to God, He has power over all things.

2.286. God does not charge a soul with more than it can bear.

2.286. (prayer)-'Our Lord, do not take us to task if we forget or make a mistake! Our Lord, do not place on us a burden like the one You placed on those before us! Our Lord, do not place on us a burden we have not the strength to bear! Pardon us; and forgive us; and have mercy on us. You are our Lord and Sustainer, so help us against those who deny the truth.'

The Family of 'Imran (Al-'Imran)

3.1. God! There is no deity save Him, the Living, the Sustainer. He has sent down the Standard by which to discern the true from the false.

3. 5. Nothing on earth or in the heavens is hidden from God.

3.26. Say, 'Lord, sovereign of all sovereignty. You bestow sovereignty on whom you will and take it away from whom You please; You exalt whoever You will and abase whoever You will. All that is good lies in Your hands. You have the power to will anything.

3.27. You cause the night to pass into the day, and the day into the night; You bring forth the living from the lifeless and the lifeless from the living. You give without measure to whom You will.

3.29. Say, 'God knows everything that is in your heart, whether you conceal it or reveal it; He knows everything that the heavens and earth contain; God has power over all things

3.31. God is most forgiving, and most merciful.

3.47. God creates what He wills: when He wills a thing He need only say, "Be," and it is.

3.51. God is my Lord and your Lord, so worship Him. That is the straight path.

3.92 Never will you attain to righteousness unless you spend for the cause of God out of what you cherish; and whatever you spend is known to God.

3.122. In God let the faithful put their trust.

3.126. help comes only from God, the Powerful, the Wise One

3.129 Whatever is in the heavens and whatever is on the earth belong to God.

3.131. Fear God, so that you may prosper

3.138 This Quran is an exposition for the people and a guidance and admonition for those who fear God.

3.139. And do not become faint of heart, nor grieve, you will have the upper hand, if you are believers.

3.144. Muhammad is only a messenger.

3.146. God loves the patient.

3.152. God is most gracious to the believers.

3.153. God is aware of what you do.

3.154. Say to them, 'All is in the hands of God.' God is aware of your innermost thoughts.

3.156. it is God who gives life and causes death. And God sees all that you do.

3.159. When you have decided upon a course of action, place your trust in God: for God loves those who place their trust in Him.

3.160 If God helps you, none can overcome you.

3.173. 'God is sufficient for us. He is the best guardian.'

Women (Al-Nisa')

4.1. God is always watching over you.

4.11. He is all knowing and all wise.

4.12. God is all knowing and forbearing.

4.26. God wishes to explain things to you and guide you to the ways of those who have gone before you and to turn to you in mercy. God is all knowing and all wise.

4.28. God wishes to lighten your burdens, for, human has been created weak.

4.32. You should rather ask God for His bounty. God has knowledge of all things.

4.33. God is witness to all things.

4.45. God suffices as a patron, and God suffices as a supporter.

4.47. God's command is always carried out.

4.45. God suffices as a patron, and God suffices as a supporter.

4.47. God's command is always carried out.

4.49. It is indeed God who purifies whoever He pleases and none shall be wronged by as much as a hair's breadth.

4.56. God is mighty and wise.

4.58. God hears and sees all things.

4.69. Whoever obeys God and the Messenger, will be among those He has blessed: the messengers, the truthful, the witnesses, and the righteous. What excellent companions these are!

4.70. Sufficient is God's infinite knowledge.

4.79. God suffices as a witness.

4.81. God is sufficient as a trustee.

4.82. Do they not ponder on the Quran? If it had been from anyone other than God, they would have found much inconsistency in it.

4.84. You are responsible only for yourself.

4. 85. Whoever rallies to a good cause shall have a share in its blessing; and whoever rallies to an evil cause shall be answerable for his part in it: for, indeed, God watches over everything.

4.86. God takes account of all things.

4.87. He is God: there is no deity other than Him. He will gather you all together on the Day of Resurrection; there is no doubt about it. Whose word can be truer than God's?

4.94. With God there are good things in plenty.

4.95. God has promised all a good reward; but far greater is the recompense of those who strive for Him.

4.99. God is ever pardoning and ever forgiving.

4.106. Ask God for forgiveness: He is most forgiving and merciful.

4.124. Anyone who performs good deeds, whether it be a man or woman, provided that s/he is a believer, shall enter Paradise. No one shall suffer the least injustice.

4.126. To God belongs all that the heavens and earth contain. God has knowledge of all things.

4.128. If you do good and fear Him, surely God is aware of what you do.

4.130. God is bountiful and wise.

4.131. All that the heavens and the earth contain belongs to God. God is self-sufficient and praiseworthy.

4.132. None is as worthy of trust as God.

4.134. If one desires the rewards of this world [let him remember that] with God are the rewards of [both] this world and the life to come: and God is indeed all hearing, all seeing.

4.135. Believers, be strict in upholding justice and bear witness for the sake of God, even though it be against yourselves, your parents, or your kindred. Be they rich or poor, God knows better about them both. Do not, then, follow your own desires, lest you swerve from justice. If you conceal the truth or evade it, then remember that God is well aware of all that you do.

4.147. God is appreciative and aware.

4.147. God hears all and knows all.

4.148. God hears all and knows all.

4.149. God is forgiving and all powerful.

4.158. God is almighty and wise.

4.171. To Him belongs whatever is in the heavens and whatever is on the earth. And God is sufficient as a guardian.

4.173. Those who believe and do good works will be fully recompensed by Him. And He will give them yet more out of His bounty;

4.174. Men, you have received clear evidence from your Lord. We have sent down a clear light to you.

4.176. God has knowledge of all things.

The Table (Al-Ma'idah)

5.1. Believers, fulfill your obligations.

5.2. Help one another in goodness and in piety.

5.4. All good things have been made lawful for you;

5.6. God does not wish to place any burden on you; He only wishes to purify you and perfect His favour to you, in order that you may be grateful.

5.8. God is aware of all that you do.

5.9. God has promised those who believe and do good deeds forgiveness and a great reward;

5.11. Have fear of God and in God let the believers place their trust.

5.13. Truly, God loves the doers of good.

5.16. God guides to the ways of peace all who seek His good pleasure,

5.17. The kingdom of the heavens and the earth and everything between them belong to God. He creates what He will and God has power over all things.

5.18. He forgives whom He pleases and punishes whom He pleases. The kingdom of the heavens and the earth and all that is between them, belong to God and all shall return to Him.

5.19. God has the power to do all things.

5.35. Believers, fear God and seek ways to come closer to Him and strive for His cause, so that you may prosper.

5.39. Surely, God is most forgiving and ever merciful.

5.40. Do you not know that the kingdom of the heavens and earth belongs to God? He punishes whom He will and forgives whom He pleases. God has power over all things.

5.42. God loves those that deal justly.

5.48. Vie, then, with one another in doing good works; to God you shall all return; then He will make clear to you about what you have been disputing.

5.50. Who is a better judge than God, for men whose faith is firm?

5.54. Such is God's bounty, which He gives to anyone He wishes. God is bountiful and all-knowing.

5.55 Your helpers are only God and His Messenger and the believers

5.56. and the believers must know that God's party is sure to triumph.

5.57. Have fear of God, if you are true believers.

5.76. God alone is the All Hearing and All Knowing.

5.77. Say, 'People of the Book! Do not go to extremes in your religion.

5.83. 'Our Lord, we believe, so count us among those who bear witness.

5.84. Why should we not believe in God and in the truth that has come down to us? We yearn for our Lord to admit us among the righteous.

5.87. Believers, do not forbid the wholesome good things, which God made lawful to you. Do not transgress; God does not love the transgressors..

5.88. Fear God, in whom you believe.

5.89. Do keep your oaths.

5.93. God loves those who do good.

5.99. God knows what you reveal and what you hide.

5.101. God is most forgiving and forbearing.

5.105. Believers, take care of your own souls.

5.120. The kingdom of the heavens and the earth and everything in them belongs to God: He has power over all things.

The Cattle (Al-An'am)

6.1. Praise be to God, who has created the heavens and the earth and brought into being darkness and light.

6.2. It is He who has created you out of clay, and then has decreed a term [for you]—a term known [only] to Him.

6.3. He is God both in the heavens and on earth, He has knowledge of all that you hide and all that you reveal. He knows what you do;

6.12. Say, 'To whom belongs all that is in the heavens and earth?' Say, 'To God. He has taken it upon Himself to be merciful. That He will gather you on the Day of Resurrection is beyond all doubt.

6.13. To Him belongs all that dwells in the night and the day. He is the All Hearing and the All Knowing.

6.14. Say, 'Shall I take as my protector someone other than God, Creator of the heavens and the earth, who feeds all and is fed by none?' Say, 'I have been commanded to be the first of those who submit.

6.15. Say, 'I will never disobey my Lord,

6.17. If He should let some good touch you, know that He has the power to do all that He wills.

6.18 He reigns Supreme over His servants; and He is the All Wise, the All Aware.

6.48.cWe send the messengers only to give good news and to warn, so those who believe and reform themselves need have no fear, nor will they grieve.

6.57. Say, 'I stand by the clear evidence from my Lord,........ Judgment is for God alone. He declares the truth. He is the best of judges.

6.59. He holds the keys to the unseen; none knows them but He. He has knowledge of all that land and sea contain. No leaf falls without His knowledge, nor is there a single grain in the darkness of the earth, or anything, wet or dry, but is recorded in a clear Record.

6.60. It is He who gathers you in at night and knows all that you do by day; then He raises you up during the day so that an appointed term may be completed. Then to Him you shall return and He will declare to you all that you used to do

6.61. He is the Absolute Master over His servants. He sends forth guardians [angels] who watch over you until, when death approaches one of you, our angels take his soul, and they never fail in their duty.

6.62. Then they will all be returned to God, their true Lord. The Judgment is His alone. He is the swiftest reckoner.

6.69. The God-fearing are not in any way held accountable for the wrongdoers; their only duty is to remind them, so that they may fear God.

6.71. Say, 'God's guidance is the only guidance. We are commanded to surrender ourselves to the Lord of the Universe.

6.72. He it is to whom you will be gathered.'

6.73. It was He who created the heavens and the earth for a true purpose. On the Day when He says, 'Be,' it shall be: His word is the truth. All sovereignty shall be His on the Day when the trumpet is sounded. The Knower of the unseen and the visible, He is the Wise, the Aware One.

6.79. I have set my face with single minded devotion, towards Him who has created the heavens and the earth, and I am not one of the polytheists.'

6.82. It is those who have faith, and do not mix their faith with wrongdoing, who will be secure, and it is they who are rightly guided.

6.83. We raise in rank anyone We please—your Lord is wise and aware.

6.88. This is the guidance of God: He gives that guidance to whichever of His servants He pleases.

6.92. This is a blessed Book which We have revealed, confirming what came before it,

6.95. It is God who splits the seed and the fruit stone. He brings forth the living from the dead, and the dead from the living. That is God. How then can you, deluded, turn away from the truth?

6.96. He causes the break of day, and has made the night for rest and He made the sun and the moon to a precise measure. That is the measure determined by the Almighty and the All Knowing.

6.97. It is He who has set up for you the stars so that you might be guided by them in the midst of the darkness of land and sea. We have made the signs clear for people who want to understand.

6.98. It is He who first produced you from a single soul, then gave you a place to stay [in life] and a resting place [after death]. We have made Our revelations clear to those who are men of understanding.

6.99. It is He who sends down water from the sky. With it We produce vegetation of all kinds; out of green foliage, We produce clustered grain; and from the date-palm, out of its sheath, We produce bunches of dates hanging low. We produce vineyards and olive groves and pomegranates, alike yet different. Look at their fruit as He causes it to grow and ripen. In this are signs for people who believe.

6.100. Hallowed be He and exalted far above what they ascribe to Him,

6.101. He created everything and is aware of everything!

6.102. This is God, your Lord, there is no God but Him, the Creator of all things, so worship Him; He is the guardian of all things.

6.103. No vision can grasp Him, but He takes in over all vision; He is the Subtle and Aware One.

6.104. Clear insights have come to you from your Lord. Whoever, therefore, chooses to see, does so for his own good; and whoever chooses to remain blind, does so to his own loss.

6.106. Follow what has been revealed to you from your Lord: there is no deity but Him; and ignore the polytheists.

6.108. To their Lord they shall all return, and He will declare to them all that they have done.

6.115. The Word of your Lord is perfected in truth and justice. None can change His words. He is the All Hearing, the All Knowing.

6.117. He knows best those who are guided.

6.119. Surely, many mislead others by their desires through lack of knowledge. But your Lord best knows the transgressors.

6.126. This is the straight path leading to your Lord. We have made the signs clear for thinking men.

6.133. Your Lord is the self sufficient One, the merciful. If He wills, He can take you away and replace you by anyone He pleases, just as He raised you from the offspring of other people.

6.134. That which you are promised shall surely come to pass and you cannot prevent it.

6.145. Your Lord is most forgiving and merciful.

6.152. We never charge a soul with more than it can bear.

6.153. [He has enjoined], 'this is My straight path; so follow it, and do not follow other ways: that will lead you away from His path.' That is what He enjoins upon you, so that you may guard yourselves.

6.155. This is a Book which We have revealed as a blessing— follow it and fear your Lord, so that you may receive mercy

6.160. Whoever does a good deed will be repaid tenfold,

6.161. Say, 'My Lord has guided me to a straight path,

6.162. Say, 'My prayer and my sacrifice and my life and my death are all for God, the Lord of the worlds;

6.163. He has no partner. So am I commanded, and I am the first of those who submit.'

6.164. Say, 'Shall I seek a lord other than God, while He is the Lord of all things?' Everyone must bear the consequence of what he does, and no bearer of a burden can bear the burden of another. Then to your Lord you will return, and He will inform you of what you used to dispute about.

The Heights (Al-A'raf)

7.2. This Book has been sent down to you—let there be no heaviness in your heart about it—so that you may warn by means of it and it is a reminder to the believers.

7.3.3 Follow what has been sent down to you by your Lord and do not follow any protector other than Him.

7.10. We established you in the land and provided you with a means of livelihood there:

7.26. But the raiment of righteousness is the best. That is one of the signs of God. So that people may take heed.

7.29. Say, 'My Lord has commanded you to act justly. Turn your faces up toward Him at every time and place of worship, and call upon Him, making yourselves sincere towards Him in religion. As He brought you into being, so shall you return'

7.42. We do not burden any soul with more than it can bear

7.52. And surely We have brought them a Book which We have expounded with knowledge, a guide and a mercy for those who believe.

7.54. His is the creation, His the command Blessed be God, Lord of the universe!

7.55. Call on your Lord with humility and in secret

7.56. do not spread corruption on the earth after it has been set in order—pray to Him with fear and hope, God's mercy is close to those who do good.

7.128. 'Turn to God for help and be patient. The earth belongs to God. He gives it to those of His servants whom He chooses, and the future belongs to the God-fearing.

7.180. God has the Most Excellent Names. Call on Him by His Names

7.199. Be tolerant; enjoin what is right; and avoid the ignorant.

7.200. seek refuge with God; He is all hearing, and all knowing.

7.205 Remember your Lord deep in your very soul, in all humility and awe, without raising your voice, morning and evening-

The Spoils of War (Al-Anfal)

8.1. So fear God, and set things right among yourselves, and obey God and His Messenger, if you are true believers:

8.2. True believers are those whose hearts tremble with awe at the mention of God, and whose faith grows stronger as they listen to His revelations. They are those who put their trust in their Lord,

8.4. Such are the true believers. They have a high standing with their Lord, His forgiveness and an honorable provision made for them.

8.10. for help comes from God alone. Surely, God is Mighty and Wise.

8.17. Surely, God is all hearing, all-knowing

8.24. Believers, obey God and the Messenger when he calls you to that which gives you life. Know that God stands between man and his heart, and you shall all be gathered in His presence.

8.28. Know that your wealth and children are a trial and that there is an immense reward with God.

8.29. Believers, if you fear God, He will grant you the ability to discriminate between right and wrong, and will forgive you your sins: for God is limitless in His great bounty.

8.30. God is the best of schemers (planner)

8.40. know that God is your Protector; the Best of Protectors and the Best of Helpers!

8.41. God has power over all things.

8.42. Surely, God is all hearing and all-knowing.

8.43. He (God) has full knowledge of what is in the human heart.

8.44. Everything returns to God.

8.45. Believers! When you encounter a party, remain firm and remember God much, so that you may succeed.

8.46. Obey God and His Messenger, and avoid dissension, lest you falter

and are no longer held in awe. Have patience: God is with those who are patient.

8.49. But he who places his trust in God [knows that], God is Almighty and Wise.

8.53. God would never withdraw a favour that He had conferred upon a people unless they change what is in their hearts. God is all hearing and all knowing.

8.60. Anything you spend in the way of God will be repaid to you in full. You will not be wronged.

8.61. and put your trust in God. Surely, it is He who is All Hearing and All Knowing.

8.62. God is enough for you: it was He who strengthened you with His help,

8.64. O Prophet! God is sufficient for you and the believers who follow you.

8.66. God has now lightened your burden, for He knows that there is weakness in you............God is with the steadfast.

8.67. You desire the gain of this world, while God desires for you the Hereafter—God is mighty and wise.

8.71. God is aware and wise.

8.72. God sees what you do.

8.74. God has full knowledge of all things.

Repentance (Al-Taw bah)

9.4. God loves those who are righteous.

9.27. God is forgiving and merciful.

9.36. and know that God is with the righteous.

9.38. But little is the comfort of this life, compared to that of the Hereafter.

9.39. God has power over all things.

9.43. May God pardon you.

9.44. God best knows the righteous.

9.51. Say, 'Nothing can befall us, except what God has ordained for us. He is our Supreme Lord. In God let the faithful put their trust.

9.59. 'God is sufficient for us. God will give us out of His bounty, and so will His Messenger. To God alone do we turn with hope!

9.71. The believers, both men and women, are friends to each other; they enjoin what is good and forbid evil, they attend to their prayers and pay the alms and obey God and His Messenger. On these God will have mercy, for God is almighty and wise.

9.72. God has promised the believers, both men and women, Gardens through which rivers flow, wherein they will abide, and fine dwelling places in Gardens of eternity. But the good pleasure of God is greater still. That is the supreme achievement.

9.98. God hears all and knows all.

9.104. 104 Do they not know that God accepts the repentance of His servants and receives their alms, and that God is the Forgiving, the Merciful One?

9.108. God loves those who purify themselves.

9.115. God would never lead a people astray after He has guided them and until He has made clear to them what they should guard against. God has knowledge of all things;

9.116. surely to God belongs the kingdom of the heavens and of the earth. He gives life and death. You have none besides God to protect or help you.

9.119. Believers, fear God and stand with the truthful.

9.120. God will not deny the righteous their reward.

9.121.and whenever they spend anything [for the sake of God], be it little or much, and whenever they traverse the land [in God's cause] it is recorded to their credit, and God will grant them the best reward for all that they have been doing.

9.123. Know that God is with those who fear Him.

9.128 There has come to you a Messenger of your own. Your suffering distresses him: he is deeply concerned for your welfare and full of kindness and mercy towards the believers.

9.129. 'God suffices me: there is no deity but He: in Him I have put my trust. He is the Lord of the Glorious Throne.

Jonah (Yunus)

10.3. Truly, your Lord is God who created the heavens and the earth in six days [periods], then He ascended the Throne, disposing the whole affair. No one may intercede with Him save with His permission. Such is God, your Lord, so worship Him alone. Will you not take heed?

10.4. To Him you shall all return. God's promise is true; He originates Creation, then He restores it, so that He may reward with justice those who believe and do good works.

10.5. God has not created all these without a purpose. He makes plain His revelations to men of understanding.

10.9. Those who believe and do good deeds will be guided by their Lord because of their faith.

10.10. 'All praise is due to God, the Lord of the Universe!'

10.25. God calls man to the home of peace and He guides whom He wills to a straight path.

10.26. Those who do good works shall have a good reward and more besides. No darkness and no ignominy shall cover their faces. They are destined for Paradise wherein they shall dwell forever.

10.31. Say, 'Who provides [sustenance] for you from heaven and earth? Who is it who controls the ears and the eyes? Who brings forth the living from the dead, and the dead from the living? And who governs all affairs?' They will say, 'God'. Then say, 'Will you not then fear Him?

10.32. That is God, your true Lord. What is there, besides the truth, but error? How then can you turn away?'

10.37. This Quran is not such as could have been produced by anyone but God. It fulfills that [the predictions] which came before it and gives a fuller explanation of the [earlier] Revelations. There is no doubt about it: it is from the Lord of the Universe.

10.41. If they should reject you, say, 'My deeds are mine and your deeds are yours. You are not accountable for my actions, nor am I accountable for what you do.'

10.44. Surely, God does not wrong people at all, but people wrong themselves.

10.47. Every nation has a messenger.

10.49. For every people, however, there is an appointed term. When the end of their term arrives, they cannot postpone it for an hour, nor can they advance it.'

10.55. Assuredly, everything that is in the heavens and on the earth belongs to God. Assuredly, God's promise is true. Yet most of them do not realize it.

10.56. He gives life and brings about death, and to Him you shall all return.

10.57. O mankind! There has come to you an admonition from your Lord, a cure for what is in the hearts, and a guide and a blessing to true believers.

10.58. Say, 'In the grace and mercy of God let them rejoice, for these are better than the worldly riches which they hoard.'

10.60. God is bountiful to humans:

10.61. In whatever activity you may be engaged, and whichever part of the Quran you recite, and whatever deed you do, We are witness to it when you are engaged in it. Not the smallest particle on the earth or in heaven is hidden from your Lord; and there is nothing smaller or bigger but is recorded in a clear Book.

10.62. Those who are close to God shall certainly have no fear, nor shall they grieve.

10.63. For those who believe and are mindful of God, 10.64. there is good news in this life and in the Hereafter: the Word of God shall never change. That is the supreme triumph.

10.65. Surely, all might and glory belongs to God alone; He is the all-hearing, the all-knowing.

10.67. It is He who has made the night dark for you so that you may rest in it and the day a source of light. Surely, there are signs in this for a people who listen.

10.68. Glory be to Him. He is the Self-Sufficient One; everything in the heavens and on the earth belongs to Him.

10.82. God establishes the truth by His words,

10.94. If you are in any doubt concerning what We have sent down to you, then question those who have read the Book before you: the Truth has come to you from your Lord, so do not be one of the doubters

10.107. If God inflicts harm on you, no one can remove it but He, and if He intends good for you, no one can withhold His bounty; He grants His bounty to any of His servants whom He will. He is the Most Forgiving, and the Most Merciful.

10.108. Say, 'Mankind, Truth has come to you from your Lord! Anyone who accepts guidance is guided only for his own sake;

10.109. Follow what is revealed to you, [O Prophet], and be steadfast until God gives His judgment. He is the Best of Judges.

Hud (Hud)

11.1. [This is] a Book, with verses which are fundamental [in nature], and then expounded in detail by One who is all wise and all aware.

11.2. [It teaches] that you should worship none but God. I am sent to you from Him to warn you and to give you good tidings.

11.3. Seek forgiveness from your Lord; then turn towards Him [in repentance]. He will make generous provision for you for an appointed term and will bestow His grace on all who merit it!

11.4. to God you shall all return; and He has power over all things.

11.6. There is not a living creature on the earth but it is for God to provide its sustenance. He knows its dwelling and its [final] resting place. All this is recorded in a clear book.

11.12. God is the guardian of all things.

11.13. know that this [Quran] is sent down with God's knowledge and that there is no deity but Him. Will you then surrender yourselves to Him?

11.23. Those who have believed and done good deeds and humbled themselves before their Lord are destined for Paradise, and they will live in it forever.

11.34. He is your Lord and you will all return to Him.

11.49. so be patient: the future belongs to the God fearing.

11.56. I have put my trust in God, my Lord and your Lord. For there is no living creature which He does not hold by its forelock. My Lord is on the straight path.

11.57. For my Lord is guardian over all things.

11.61. My Lord is near and responsive.'

11.66. Surely, your Lord is powerful and mighty.

11.86. What God leaves with you is the best for you, if you are believers.

11.90. Seek forgiveness of your Lord and turn to Him in repentance. For my Lord is indeed merciful and loving.

11.92. Surely, my Lord encompasses all that you do.

11.112. Therefore stand firm [in the straight path] as you are commanded, along with those who have turned to God with you, and do not exceed the bounds, for He sees everything you do.

11.115. Be steadfast; for surely, God does not let the wages of the righteous be wasted.

11.117. Your Lord would never unjustly destroy communities while their people were trying to reform.

11.119. The word of your Lord shall be fulfilled.

11.123. The knowledge of the secret of the heavens and the earth belongs to God alone, and to Him shall all affairs be referred. So worship Him and put your trust in Him alone. Your Lord is not unaware of what you do.

Joseph (Yusuf)

12.1. These are verses from the clear Book.

12.2. We have sent down the Quran in Arabic, so that you may understand.

12.3. We recount to you the best of narratives in revealing this Quran to you, even though you were unaware of it before it came.

12. 6. You shall be chosen by your Lord and He will impart to you some understanding of the inner meaning of events. He will bestow the full measure of His blessings upon you......Truly, your Sustainer is all-knowing and wise!'

12.18. But it is best to be patient:

12.21. God has power over all things. However, most people do not know this.

12.22. We reward those who do good.

12.23. Wrongdoers certainly never prosper.'

12.34. He is All Hearing and All Knowing.

12.38.it is not for us to associate anyone with God as a partner. This is of God's grace upon us and upon mankind; even though most men are not

grateful.

12.39. ….Are many diverse lords better, or God, the One, the Almighty?

12.40. All those you worship instead of Him are mere names you and your forefathers have invented, names for which God has sent down no authority: all power belongs to God alone, and He orders you to worship none but Him: this is the true faith, though most people do not realize it.

12.53. Indeed, my Lord is forgiving and merciful.

12.56. We (God) bestow Our mercy on whomever We please, and We do not allow the reward of the righteous to go to waste.

12.57. Yet the reward of the hereafter is best for those who believe and are mindful of God.

12.64. But God is the best of guardians, the Most Merciful of all.'

12.67. I cannot help you in any way against God; judgement is His alone. In Him I have put my trust. In Him let the faithful put their trust.

12.67. We (God) exalt whoever We please: but above those who have knowledge there is One all knowing.

12.86. 'I only complain of my anguish and my sorrow to God.

12.87. Do not despair of God's mercy; none but those who deny the truth despair of God's mercy.

12.88. Truly, God rewards the charitable.'

12.90. The truth is that God does not waste the reward of those who do good, who are righteous and steadfast.'

12.92. May God forgive you! And He is the Most Merciful of those who show mercy.

12.100. My Lord is the best planner in achieving what He will; He is All Knowing, and Truly Wise.'

12.101. Creator of the heavens and the earth, You are my patron in this world and the Hereafter! Make me die in submission to You and admit me among the righteous.'

12.105. And there are many signs in the heavens and the earth that they pass by and give no heed to—12.106. and most of them, even when they profess belief in God, attribute partners to Him.

12.111. This [Quran] is no invented tale, but a confirmation of the previous [scripture] and a detailed explanation of all things as well as guidance and mercy to true believers.

Thunder (Al-Ra'D)

13.1. These are the verses of the Book. What is sent down to you from your Lord is the truth, yet most men do not believe in it.

13.2. It was God who raised the heavens with no visible supports, and then established Himself on the throne; He has regulated the sun and the moon, so that each will pursue its course for an appointed time; He ordains all things and makes plain His revelations, so that you may be certain of meeting your Lord;

13.6. Your Lord is full of forgiveness for mankind, despite their wrongdoings,

13.7. Every people has its guide.

13.8. God knows what every female bears. He knows of every change within the womb. For everything He has a proper measure;

13.9. He is the knower of the unseen and the visible, the Great, the Most-Exalted.

13.10. It makes no difference whether you converse in secret or aloud, whether you hide under the cloak of night or walk about freely in the light of day.

13.11. God does not change the condition of a people's lot, unless they change what is in their hearts.

13.12. It is He who shows you the lightning, inspiring fear and hope, and gathers up the heavy clouds; 13. 13. and the thunder glorifies Him with His praise and the angels do so too in awe of Him, and He sends His thunderbolts to strike anyone He pleases, yet they dispute about God, who is inexorable in His power.

13.14. The only true appeal is to God alone;

13.15. All who dwell in heavens and on the earth submit to God alone, willingly or unwillingly, as do their shadows in the mornings and in the evenings.

13.16. Say, 'God is the Creator of all things. He is the One, the Almighty.'

13.18. There will be the best of rewards for those who respond to their Lord:

13.19. Can one who knows that whatever has been sent down to you from your Lord is the Truth, be equal to one who is blind? It is only those who are endowed with insight who pay heed;

13.20. they who are true to their bond with God and never break their covenant; 13.21. and those who join together what God has commanded to be joined, and fear their Lord and dread the harshness of the reckoning;

13.22. Those who are steadfast in seeking the favour of their Lord, and pray regularly and spend secretly and openly out of what We have provided them with, and ward off evil with good. Theirs shall be the final abode.

13.23. They shall enter the eternal Gardens of Eden,

13.24. how excellent is the final abode!'

13.26 God gives abundantly to whom He will and sparingly to whom He pleases—[those who deny the truth] rejoice in the life of this world; yet the life of this world is but a fleeting pleasure compared with the life to come.

13.27. (God) guides to Himself those who turn to Him,

13.28. those who believe and whose hearts find comfort in the remembrance of God—surely in the remembrance of God hearts can find comfort.

13.29. 'As for those who believe and do righteous deeds—blissful is their end.'

13.30. Say, 'He is my Lord; there is no god but He. In Him I put my trust and to Him I shall return.'

13.31. Surely all things are subject to God's will......... God will not fail to keep His promise.

13.33. Is then He who watches over every soul and its actions [like any other]?

13.36. Say to them, 'I have been commanded only to worship God and not to associate partners with Him: to Him I pray and to Him I shall return.

13.39. God abrogates or confirms what He pleases; with Him is the source of all commandments.

13.41. God decides—no one can reverse His decision—and He is swift in reckoning.

13.42. but in all things the master planning is God's. He knows what each soul does. Those who deny the truth shall soon know for whom is the final abode.

Abraham (Ibrahim)

14.1. We have revealed to you this Book so that, by their Lord's command, you may lead men from darkness to the light: to the path of the Mighty, the Praiseworthy One, 14.2. to God, who possesses whatever is in the heavens and whatever is on earth.

14.4. He is the Almighty, the All Wise.

14.8. God is self-sufficient, praiseworthy.'

14.11. In God let true believers put their trust.

14.12........So in God let those who trust put their trust.'

14.19. Do you not see that God has created the heavens and the earth for a purpose? He can eliminate you if He wills and bring into being a new creation: 14.20. that is no difficult thing for God.

14.23. But those who believed and did good deeds will be brought into Gardens with rivers flowing through them. They shall abide there forever by their Lord's permission, and will be welcomed with the greeting, 'Peace'!

14.27. God will strengthen the believers with His steadfast word, both in the present life and in the Hereafter.

14.38. Lord, You have knowledge of all that we hide and all that we reveal: nothing in heaven or on earth is hidden from God........ Surely my Lord is the hearer of prayer.

14.40. Lord, grant that I may keep up the prayer, and so may my offspring. My Lord, accept my prayer.

14.41. Forgive me, Lord, and forgive my parents and all the believers on the Day of Reckoning.'

14.47. Never think that God will fail in His promise to His messengers. God is mighty.

14.52. This is a message for mankind. Let them take warning from it and know that He is but one God. Let those possessed of understanding may take heed.

The Rocky Tract (Al-Hijr)

15.1. These are the verses of a clear Book, the Quran.

15.9. It is We who have sent down the Reminder (Quran) and We will, most surely, safeguard it.

15. 23. Truly, it is We who bring to life and We who cause death and We are the inheritor of all things.

15.24. We know those who lived before you and those who will come after you.

15.25. It is your Lord who will gather them. He is all wise and all knowing.

15.49 Tell My servants that I alone am the Forgiving, the Merciful One,

15.86 Surely your Lord is the All Knowing Creator!

15.98. But glorify your Lord with His praise, and prostrate yourself:

15.99. and worship your Lord until what is certain [death] comes to you.

Bees (Al-Nahl)

16. 1. The decree of God is at hand, so do not seek to hasten it. Holy is He, and exalted far above what they associate with Him.

16.2. He sends down the angels with revelations by His command to whoever of His servants He pleases, saying, 'Warn mankind that there is no god save Me, so fear Me.'

16.3. He created the heavens and the earth for a true purpose. He is exalted above anything they associate with Him.

16.7. Surely, your Lord is compassionate and merciful.

16.8. He creates other things beyond your knowledge.

16.9 The straightway leads to God and there are ways which deviate from the right course.

16.17. Is He, then, who creates like him who does not create? Will you not, then, take heed?

16.18. If you tried to count God's blessings, you would never be able to number them. God is ever forgiving and most merciful.

16.19. God knows all that you conceal and all that you reveal.

16.20. Those you call on besides God cannot create anything. They are themselves created.

16.21. They are dead, not living; nor do they know when they will be raised to life.

16.22. Your God is the One God.

16.23. God surely knows what they conceal and what they reveal. He does not love the arrogant.

16.28. 'God is aware of what you have been doing,

16.30 When those who fear God are asked, 'What has your Lord sent down?' Their reply is, 'Goodness!' The reward of those who do good works in this world is good, but the abode of the Hereafter is even better. The home of the righteous is indeed excellent.

16.31. They will enter Gardens of Eternity, where rivers will flow at their feet. There they will have all that they wish for. Thus God rewards the righteous,

16.40. When We (God) will something to happen, all that We say is, 'Be!' and it is.

16.51. God says, 'Do not take two gods. He is only One God. So fear Me alone.'

16.52. To Him belongs whatsoever is in the heavens and on the earth, and obedience is due to Him alone. Will you then fear anyone other than God?

16.53. Whatever blessing you have is from God, and to Him you turn for help when distress befalls you,

while to

16.60. God applies the highest attribute, for He is Mighty, the Wise.

16.74. Do not compare God with anyone. God has knowledge, but you have not.

16.77. God alone has knowledge of the hidden reality of the heavens and the earth; and the coming of the Hour [of Judgement] is like the twinkling of an eye, or even quicker. Surely God has full power over everything.

16.81......Thus He completes His favour to you, so that you may submit wholly to Him.

16.82. But if they turn away, you are responsible only for conveying the message clearly.

16.89. We have sent down the Book to you to make everything clear, a guidance, and a mercy, and glad tidings for those who submit to God.

16.90. God commands justice, kindness and giving their [due to] near relatives, and He forbids all shameful deeds, and injustice and transgression. He admonishes you so that you may take heed!

16.92......God is only testing you by means of this. On the Day of Resurrection He will make it clear to you what you differed about.

16.94. What is with God is better for you if you only knew.

12.96. What you have shall pass away, but what is with God is lasting. We will certainly give those who are patient their reward according to the best of their actions.

16.97. To whoever does good deeds, man or woman, and is a believer, We shall assuredly give a good life; and We will bestow upon them their reward according to the best of their works.

16.98. When you read the Quran, seek God's protection from Satan, the rejected one. 16.99. Surely, he has no power over those who believe and put their trust in their Lord; 16.100. he has power only over those who are willing to follow him and associate others with God.

16.102. Say, 'The Holy Spirit has brought it (Quran) down as truth from your Lord, so that He may strengthen those who believe, and also as guidance and as good tidings for those who submit.'

16.110. Surely, your Lord will be forgiving and merciful towards those who migrated after persecution and strove hard for the cause of God and remained steadfast.

16.114. So eat the lawful and good things which God has provided for you, and be thankful for the blessing of God, if it is Him you worship.

16.119. Surely, your Lord is most forgiving and ever merciful towards those who do evil in ignorance and truly repent thereafter and make amends.

16.125. Call to the way of your Lord with wisdom and fair exhortation and reason with them in a way that is best. Your Lord knows best those who have strayed away from His path, and He knows best those who are rightly guided.

16.127. Endure with patience; truly, your patience is possible only with the help of God.

16.128. for God is with those who are righteous and those who do good.

The Night Journey (Al-Isra')

17.9. Surely, this Quran guides to the most upright way and gives good news to the believers who do good deeds, so that they will have a great reward.

17.15. Who ever chooses to follow the right path, follows it for his own good; and whoever goes astray, goes astray at his own peril; no bearer of burdens shall bear the burdens of another.

17.19. Anyone who desires the Hereafter and makes a proper effort to achieve it, being a true believer, shall find favour with God for his endeavors.

17.20. Upon all, both these [who desire the world] and those [who desire the Hereafter] We bestow the bounty of your Lord: non shall be denied the bounty of your Lord—

17.21. see how We have exalted some above others [in the present life]. Yet the Hereafter shall be greater in degrees of rank and greater in excellence.

17.22. Do not set up any other deity beside God, lest you incur disgrace, and be forsaken.

17.23. Your Lord has commanded that you should worship none but Him, and show kindness to your parents.

17.25. Your Lord knows best what is in your hearts; if you are righteous, He is most forgiving to those who constantly turn to Him.

17.36. Do not follow what you do not know; for the ear and the eye and the heart shall all be called to account.

17.37. Do not walk proudly on the earth. You cannot cleave the earth, nor can you rival the mountains in height.

17.38. All that is evil in the sight of your Lord, and is detestable.

17.39. This is part of the wisdom that your Lord has revealed to you.

17.41. We have explained [the truth] in this Quran in various ways,

17.43. Glory be to Him! Exalted above all that they say!

17.44. The seven heavens and the earth and all who dwell therein glorify Him. There is not a single thing but glorifies Him with His praise; but you do not understand their glorification. Truly, He is forbearing and most forgiving.

17.54. Your Lord is fully aware of you. He may show you mercy if He will,

17.82. We send down in the Quran that which is healing and a mercy to those who believe,

17.87. His favours towards you has been great indeed.

17.89. In this Quran, We have set out all kinds of examples for people,

17.96. Say, 'God suffices as a witness between me and you [all]. He is informed about and observant of His servants.'

17.97. Those whom God guides are the truly guided,

17.105. We have revealed the Quran with the truth, and with the truth it has come down. We have sent you forth only to give good news and to give warning—

17.106. We have revealed the Quran bit by bit so that you may recite it to the people slowly and with deliberation. We have imparted it by gradual revelation.

17.108. Our Lord's promise is bound to be fulfilled."

17.110. Say, 'Whether you call on God or on the Merciful One: His are the finest names.'

17.111... and say, 'All praise is due to God who has never begotten a son and who has no partner in His kingdom; nor does anyone aid Him because of any weakness of His. Proclaim His greatness.'

The Cave (Al-Kahf)

18.1. Praise be to God who has sent down to His servant—the Book, which is free from any ambiguity 18.2. and which rightly directs, to give warning of stern punishment from Him, and to proclaim to the believers who do righteous deeds that they shall have an excellent recompense, 18.3. Wherein they will remain [in a state of bliss] forever.

18.14...'Our Lord is the Lord of the heavens and the earth. Never shall we call upon any deity other than Him: for that would be an outrageous thing to do.

18.15.....Who is more wicked than the man who invents a falsehood against God?

18.16....your Lord will extend His mercy to you and will make fitting provision for you in your situation.'

18.17...He whom God guides is rightly guided;

18.23. Never say of anything, 'I shall certainly do this tomorrow,' 18.24. without [adding], "if God so wills." Remember your Lord whenever you might forget and say, 'I trust my Lord will guide me to that which is even nearer to the right path than this.'

18.26. Only God has knowledge of the unseen in the heavens and on the earth. How well He sees and how well He hears! Man has no other guardian besides Him. He allows none to share His sovereignty.

18.27. Proclaim what has been revealed to you from your Lord's Book. None can change His words. You shall find no refuge besides Him.

18.28. Keep yourself attached to those who call on their Lord, morning and evening, seeking His pleasure; and do not let your eyes turn away from them, desiring the attraction of worldly life; and do not obey one whose heart We have made heedless of Our remembrance, one who pursues his own whims and becomes dissolute.

18.29. Say, 'This is the truth from your Lord. Let him who will, believe in it, and him who will, deny it.'

18.30. As for those who believe and do good deeds—We do not let the reward of anyone who does a good deed go to waste—

18.38. But as far as I am concerned, God alone is my Lord and I set up no partners with Him.

18.39. "That which God wills [will surely come to pass], there is no power save with God?"

18.44. The only support is from God, the True God. He is the best in rewarding and the best in respect of the final outcome.

18.46. Wealth and children are an ornament of the life of this world. But deeds of lasting merit are better rewarded by your Lord and a far better source of hope.

18. 54. We have explained in various ways in this Quran, for the benefit of mankind, all kinds of examples,

18.55. Nothing prevents people from believing when they are given guidance or from asking forgiveness of their Lord,

18.56. We only send the messengers to bring good news and to give warning.

18.58. Your Lord is the Forgiving One, the possessor of mercy.

18.107. Those who believe and do good works shall have the gardens of Paradise for their abode. 18.108. They shall forever dwell in the Gardens of Paradise, desiring no change.

18.109. Tell them, 'If the ocean became ink for writing the words of my Lord, surely the ocean would be exhausted before the words of my Lord came to an end—even if We were to add another ocean to it.'

18.110. Say, 'I am only a human being like yourselves. It is revealed to me that your God is One God. So let him who hopes to meet his Lord do good deeds and let him associate no one else in the worship of his Lord.'

Mary (Maryam)

19.33. Glory be to Him! He is far above that: when He decrees something, He says only, 'Be!' and it is.

19.36. God is my Lord and your Lord, so worship Him alone. That is the right path.

19.60. except for those who repent and believe and do good deeds. These will enter Heaven, and they will not be wronged in the least. 19.61. Theirs shall be the Gardens of Eden, which the All Merciful has promised to His servants without their having seen them, and most surely His promise shall be fulfilled.

19.62. They will not hear therein anything vain, only greetings of peace. They will receive their provision there morning and evening

19.63. That is the Garden which We will grant to those of Our servants who have been God-fearing.

19.64....What is before us and behind us and all that lies between belong to Him. Your Lord is not forgetful.

19.65. He is the Lord of the heavens and of the earth and of all that is between the two. So worship Him alone and be steadfast in His worship. Do you know of anyone equal to Him in His attributes?

19.76. God increases His guidance to those who follow guidance; and lasting good works are better in the sight of your Lord and are most rewarding.

19.85. The Day will surely come when We shall gather the God-fearing like [honored] guests before the Compassionate God.

19.96. The Lord of Mercy will bestow affection upon those who believe and perform righteous deeds.

19.97. We have made it [the Quran] easy, in your own language [Prophet], so that you may convey glad news to the righteous

Ta Ha (Ta Ha)

20.2. We have not sent the Quran down to you to distress you, 20.3. but only as an exhortation for him who fears God;

20.4. it is a revelation from Him who has created the earth and the high heavens,

20.5. the All Merciful settled on the throne.

20.6. To Him belongs whatever is in the heavens and whatever is on the earth, and whatever lies in between them, and all that lies under the ground.

20.7. Whether you speak aloud [or in a low voice], He hears all, for He knows your secrets and what is even more hidden.

20.8. God, there is no deity but Him. His are the most excellent names.

20.14. I am God. There is no deity save Me; so worship Me alone, and say your prayers in My remembrance. 20.15. The Hour is coming. But I choose to keep it hidden, so that every human being may be recompensed in accordance with his labors. 20.16. Do not let anyone who does not believe in it and follows his own desires turn you away from it and so bring you to ruin.'

20.25. 'My Lord! Open up my heart, 20.26. and make my task easy for me. 20.27. Loosen the knot in my tongue, 20.28. so that they may understand my speech, 20.29. and appoint for me a helper from among my family,

20.82. But I am most forgiving towards him who turns in repentance and believes and acts righteously and follows the right path.'

20.98. Your only deity is God, there is no deity but Him. His knowledge encompasses all things.'

20.99...We have given you a reminder [the Quran] from Us.

20.113. We have thus sent down the Quran in Arabic and given all kinds of warnings in it, so that they may fear God, or may take heed—

20.114. exalted is God, the True King. Do not be impatient with the Quran before its revelation is completed, and say, 'My Lord, increase my knowledge.'

20.131. Do not regard with envy the worldly benefits We have given some of them, for with these We seek only to test them. The provision of your Lord is better and more lasting.

20.132. Bid your people say their prayers, and be constant in their observance. We demand nothing from you. It is We who provide for you, and the best end is that of righteousness.

The Prophets (Al-Anbiya')

21.4. Say, 'My Lord knows every word spoken in the heavens and on the earth. He is All Hearing, All Knowing.'

21.10. We have revealed a Book to you which is admonition for you. Will you not then understand?

21.19. To Him belongs whosoever is in the heavens and on the earth and those that are with Him are never too proud to worship Him, nor do they grow weary;

21.20. they glorify Him night and day without tiring.

21.23. None shall question Him about His works, but they shall be questioned.

21.25. We sent all messengers before you with this revelation: 'There is no deity save Me, so worship Me alone.'

21.35. Every soul shall taste death; We test you with both good and evil [circumstances] as a trial. To Us you shall return.

21.47. We shall set up scales of justice on the Day of Resurrection, so that no soul can be in the least wronged. Actions as small as a grain of mustard seed shall be weighed. We are sufficient as a reckoner.

21.49. those who fear their Lord in the unseen, also dread the Hour of Judgement.

21.50. This is a blessed reminder that We have revealed to you. Will you

then reject it?

21.81. For it is We who have knowledge of all things—

21.87. 'There is no deity but You. Glory be to You! I was indeed wrong.'

21.92 This community of yours is one community and I am your Lord, so worship Me.

21.94. He who does good works while he is a believer, shall not see his efforts disregarded: We record them all.

21.104. On that Day We shall roll up the heavens like a scroll of parchment. As We originated the first creation, so shall We repeat it. This is a promise binding on Us. Truly, We shall fulfill it.

21.105. We have already written in the Psalms following the Reminder, 'My righteous servants shall inherit the earth.'

21.106. Herein, surely is a message for true worshippers.

21.107. We have sent you forth as a mercy to all mankind.

21.108. Say, 'It has been revealed to me that your God is but One God. Will you then submit to Him?'

21.110. God surely knows what you say openly and also knows what you conceal.

21.112. Say, 'My Lord, judge with truth. Our Lord is the Gracious One whose help we seek....

The Pilgrimage (*Al-Hajj*)

22.6...... that is because God is the truth. It is He who gives life to the dead and He has the power to will anything.

22.10....God is not unjust to His servants.'

22.16. We have sent down the Quran as clear evidence, and surely God guides whom He will.

22.17.....Surely God is witness to everything.

22.18......Surely, God does what He wills.

22.31. Devote yourselves to God, not associating any partners with Him.

22.34.....Your God is One God; surrender yourselves to Him; and give good news to the humble 22.35. whose hearts are filled with awe at the mention of God; who endure adversity with fortitude, say their prayers regularly and spend out of what We have given them.

22.38. God will surely defend the believers.

22.40......God will surely help him who helps His cause—God is indeed powerful and mighty.

22.41......The final outcome of all affairs rests with God.

22.46.......the truth is that it is not the eyes that are blind but the hearts that are in the bosoms that are blinded.

22.47......A Day with your Lord is like a thousand years in your reckoning.

22.50..... Those who believe and do good deeds shall be forgiven and shall receive an honorable provision.

22.54.....God will surely guide the faithful to a straight path.

22.56.....Those who believe and do good deeds shall enter the Gardens of Bliss,

22.58.....Surely God is the Best of Providers.

22.59......For God is all knowing and most forbearing.

22.60.....God is merciful and forgiving.

22.61....God is all hearing and all seeing.

22.62.....God is the Sublime, the Great One.

22.63.....God is unfathomable, and all aware;

22. 64. all that is in the heavens and on the earth belongs to Him. Surely, God is self sufficient and praiseworthy.

22.66. it is He who gave you life. Then He will cause you to die. Then He will give you life again.

22.68. 'God is well aware of what you do.'

22.70. Do you not know that God has knowledge of what the heavens and the earth contain? All is recorded in a Book; all this is easy for God.

22.75....God is all hearing and all seeing:

22.76. He knows what lies ahead of them and what is behind them. All things shall return to God.

22.77. You who are true believers, kneel and prostrate yourselves, worship your Lord and do good works, so that you may succeed.

22.78. Strive for the cause of God as it behoves you to strive for it. He has chosen you and laid on you no burden in the matter of your religion,....... And hold fast to God. He is your master. An excellent master and an excellent helper!

The Believers (Al-Mu'minun)

23.1. Successful indeed are the believers; 23.2. those who are humble in their prayer; 23.3. those who turn away from all that is frivolous; 23.4. those who pay the *zakat*; 23.5. those who safeguard their chastity. 23.6. except with their wives, and what their right hands possess— for then they are free from blame, 23.7. but those who seek to go beyond that are transgressors—23.8. those who are faithful to their trusts and promises; 23.9. and those who attend to their prayers; 23.10. these are the heirs of Paradise 23.11. they shall abide in it forever.

23.14. ......glory be to God, the best of creators.

23.17....We have never been unmindful of Our creation.

23.43....... no community can advance or postpone its appointed time.

23.51. Messengers, eat what is wholesome and do good deeds: I am well aware of what you do.

23.52. Your religion is but one religion—and I am your only Lord, therefore, fear Me.

23.57 Those who tremble with fear of their Lord; 23.58. and believe in His messages 23.59. and do not ascribe partners to Him; 23.60. and those who give to others what has been bestowed upon them with their hearts trembling at the thought that they must return to their Lord; 23.61. it is they who vie with one another in doing good works and shall be the foremost in doing so.

23.62. We charge no soul with more than it can bear. We have a record which clearly shows the truth and they will not be wronged.

23.72. ...But the reward of your Lord is the best, for He is the Best of Providers,

23.79. He it is who has multiplied you on the earth and to Him you shall all be gathered:

23.80. He is the One who gives life and causes death and He controls the alternation of night and day. Will you not then understand?

23.84. Say, 'To whom do the earth and all therein belong? Tell me, if you have any knowledge?' 23.85. They will say, 'To God.' Say, 'So will you not pay heed? 23.86. Say, 'Who is the Lord of the seven heavens, and of the Glorious Throne?' 23.87. They will say, 'They belong to

God.' Say, 'So do you not fear Him?' 23.88. Say, 'In whose hands lies sovereignty over all things, protecting all, while none can seek protection against Him? Tell me, if you have any knowledge.' 23.89. They will say, 'All this belongs to God.' Say to them, 'How are you then deluded?'

23.91. God has not taken to Himself a son, nor is there any other deity besides Him; otherwise, each god would have walked away with what he had created. They would surely have tried to overcome one another. Glory be to God, above all that they ascribe to Him. 23.92. Knower of the unseen and the visible; He is exalted above all that which they associate with Him.

23.96. Repel evil with what is best.

23.109. Among My servants, there were those who said, "Lord, We believe, so forgive us and have mercy on us. You are the best one to show mercy."

23.115. 'Do you imagine that We created you without any purpose and that you would not be brought back to Us?'

23.116. Then, exalted be God, the true King, there is no deity except Him, the Lord of the Glorious Throne.

23.118. Say, 'Lord, forgive us and have mercy. You are the best of those who show mercy.'

Light (Al-Nur)

24.5....truly God is forgiving and merciful.

24.10.......and God is wise, acceptor of repentance.

24.18. God explains the commandments to you. God is all knowing and wise.

24.19........ God knows, and you do not know.

24.20. But for the grace of God and His mercy upon you, and were not God compassionate and merciful, [you would have come to grief].

24.22.......Let them forgive and overlook. Do you not wish God to forgive you? God is forgiving and merciful.

24.28.....God knows well what you do.

24.29.....God knows all that you do openly, and all that you would conceal.

24.30. Tell believing men to lower their gaze and remain chaste. That is purer for them. God is aware of what they do.

24.31. Say to believing women that they should lower their gaze and remain chaste and not to reveal their adornments—save what is normally apparent thereof, and they should fold their shawls over their bosoms.

24.31.....Believers, turn to God, every one of you, so that you may prosper.

24.32.....God will provide for them from His bounty, for God's bounty is infinite and He is all knowing.

24.34. We have sent down clear revelations to you and the example of those who passed away before you and an admonition for the God fearing.

24.35. God is the light of the heavens and the earth........ God has full knowledge of everything.

24.38..... so that God may reward them according to the best of their deeds and give them more out of His bounty. God provides for whoever He wills without measure.

24.41. do you not see that all those who are in the heavens and on earth praise God, as do the birds with wings outstretched? Each knows his own mode of prayer and glorification: God has full knowledge of all that they do.

24.42. To God belongs the kingdom of the heavens and the earth, and to God shall all things return.

24.44. God alternates the night and the day—truly, in this there is a lesson for men of insight.

24.45. God created every creature from water....... He has power over all things.

24.46. We have sent down revelations clearly showing the truth. God guides whom He wills to the straight path.

24.52. those who obey God and His Messenger, and fear God, and are mindful of their duty to Him, are the ones who will triumph.

24.53.....Say, 'Do not swear: your obedience, not your oaths, will count. God is well aware of all your actions.'

24.54. Obey God and obey the Messenger. If you turn away, then he is responsible for what he is charged with and you are responsible for what you are charged with. If you obey him, you will be rightly guided. The Messenger is responsible only for delivering the message clearly.

24.55. God has promised to those among you who believe and do good works that He will surely grant them power in the land as He granted to those who were before them; and that He will surely establish for them their religion which He has chosen for them. He will cause their state of fear to be replaced by a sense of security. Let them worship Me and associate no other with Me.

24.58. Thus God makes clear to you His revelations: God is all knowing and wise.

24.59. Thus God expounds to you His revelations: God is all knowing and wise.

24.61..... salute one another with a greeting of peace, a greeting from your Lord full of blessings and purity. Thus does God expound to you His commandments, so that you may understand.

24.62. They only are true believers who believe in God and His Messenger.

24.64. Surely, whatever is in the heavens and on the earth belongs to God. God knows well what condition you are in. On the Day when they return to Him, He will declare to them all that they have done. God has full knowledge of all things.

The Criterion (Al-Furqan)

25.1. Blessed be He who has revealed the criterion [the Quran] to His servant that he may warn the nations. 25.2. Sovereign of the heavens and the earth, who has begotten no children and who has no partner in His sovereignty, it is He who has created all things and measured them out precisely.

25.6. Say to them, 'It has been revealed by Him who knows every secret that is in the heavens and on the earth. Truly, He is most forgiving and most merciful.'

25.15. Say, 'Which is better, this or the Paradise of immortality which the righteous have been promised? It is their recompense and their destination.' 25.16. Abiding there forever, they shall find in it all that they desire. This is a binding promise which your Lord has made.

25.31. your Lord is sufficient as a guide and a helper.

25.47. It is He who made the night a mantle for you, and sleep for repose; and made the day a time for rising.

25.48. It is He who sends the winds as heralds of His mercy and We send down pure water from the sky

25.54 It is He who has created human beings from water

25.56. We have sent you only as a bearer of glad tidings and as a warner

25.58. Put your trust in the One who is the Ever-Living [God], who never dies, and glorify Him with His praise. He is fully aware of the sins of His servants;

25.59. it is He who created the heavens and the earth and all that is between them in six Days [periods],

25.63. The true servants of the Gracious One are those who walk upon the earth with humility....

The Poets (Al-Shu'Ara')

26.2. These are the verses of the Book that makes things clear.

26.9. truly, your Lord is the Mighty One, the Merciful.

26.78. It is He who guides me; 26.79. He who gives me food and drink; 26.80. He who cures me when I am ill; 26.81. He who will cause me to die and bring me back to life; 26.82. and He who will, I hope, forgive me my faults on the Day of the Judgement.

26.83. My Lord, bestow wisdom upon me; unite me with the righteous; 26.84. give me a good name among later generations; 26.85. and make me one of the inheritors of the Garden of Bliss;....... 26.87. and do not disgrace me on the Day when all people are resurrected,

26.104. surely, your Lord is the Mighty One, the Merciful.

26.192 This surely is a revelation from the Lord of the Universe:

The Ants (Al-Naml)

27.1....These are verses from the Quran, a book that makes things clear; 27.2. it is guidance and good news for the believers

27.6. You have received this Quran from One who is all-wise, all-knowing.

27.8. Glory be to God, Lord of the Universe!

27.11. as for those who do wrong and then do good after evil, I am most forgiving, most merciful.

27.26. He is God: there is no deity but He, the Lord of the mighty throne.'

27.40. 'This is by the grace of my Lord, to test whether I am grateful or

ungrateful. Whosoever is grateful, it is for the good of his own self; and whosoever is ungrateful, then surely my Lord is self-sufficient and generous.'

27.59. Say, 'All praise be to God, and peace be upon those servants of His whom He has chosen. Is God better, or what they associate with Him?

27.73. Truly, your Lord is bountiful to mankind,

27.88. Such is the work of God, who has ordered all things to perfection: He is fully aware of what you do.

27.89. Whoever does a good deed, shall be rewarded with what is better,

27.93. Then say, 'Praise be to God! He will show you His signs and you will recognize them. Your Lord is not unaware of what you do.'

The Story (Al-Qasas)

28.2. These are verses from the Book that makes things clear.

28.24. 'Lord, I am truly in need of whatever blessing You may send down for me,'

28.46. but We have sent you (Muhammad) as a mercy from your Lord, so that you may warn people to whom no warner has been sent before you, so that they may take heed,

28.56. You cannot guide whoever you please: it is God who guides whom He will. He best knows those who would accept guidance.

28.60. Whatever you are given in this life is nothing but a temporary provision of this life and its glitter; what God has is better and more lasting.

28.70. He is God: there is no god but Him. All Praise is due to Him in this world and the hereafter. His is the Judgement and to Him you shall be returned.

28.73.....truth belongs to God alone.......

28.82.....It is indeed God alone who gives abundantly to whom He will and sparingly to whom He pleases.......

28.83......The righteous shall have a blessed end.

28.84. He who does good shall be rewarded with something better.

28.87.....Call people to your Lord....

28.88. Invoke no god other than God, for there is no god but Him. All things are bound to perish except Himself. His is the judgement, and to Him you shall be returned.

The Spider (Al-'Ankabut)

29.6. And whoever strives, strives only for himself— God is independent of all His creation.

29.9. We shall surely admit those who believe and do good deeds to the company of the righteous.

29.44.....God has created the heavens and the earth for a purpose;

29.45.....God has knowledge of all your actions.

29.49. But the Quran is a revelation that is clear to the hearts of those endowed with knowledge.

29.56. My servants who believe, My earth is vast, so worship Me alone. 29.57. Every soul shall taste death and then to Us you shall return.

29.62. God gives abundantly to whom He will and sparingly to whom He pleases. God has full knowledge of all things.

29.69. We will surely guide in Our ways those who strive hard for Our cause, God is surely with the righteous.

The Romans (Al-Rum)

30.4. with God rests all power of decision, first and last.

30.5. He helps whom He pleases: He is the Mighty, and the Merciful.

30.6. [This is] God's promise. Never does God fail to fulfill His promise.

30.8. God has created the heavens and the earth and all that is between them for a purpose and for an appointed time.

30.11. God originates the creation, and shall repeat it, then to Him you shall be returned.

30.17. So glorify God in the evening and in the morning, 30.18. and praise be to Him in the heavens and on the earth—and glorify Him in the late afternoon, and at midday.

30.19. He brings forth the living from the dead and the dead from the living. He gives life to the earth after its death, and you shall be raised to life in the same way.

30.26. All those in the heavens and on the earth belong to Him. All are obedient to Him.

30.27. He is the One who originates creation, then repeats it, and it is very easy for Him. His is the most exalted state in the heavens and on the earth; He is the Mighty, the Wise One.

30.30. Devote yourself single mindedly to the Religion. And follow the nature [constitution] as made by God, that nature in which He has created mankind. There is no altering the creation of God. That is the right religion.

30.31. Turn to Him and fear Him, and be steadfast in prayer.....

30.40. God is He who created you, then provides for you, then will cause you to die and then bring you back to life.

30.45. For then He will reward out of His bounty those who believe and do good deeds.

30.54. He creates whatever He wishes; He is the All Knowing and All Powerful.

Luqman (Luqman)

31.2. These are the verses of the Book of wisdom, 30.3. a guide and a mercy for those who do good,

31.8. Surely, those who believe and do good works shall enter gardens of bliss, 31.9. wherein they will abide forever. That is God's true promise; He is the Mighty, the Wise One.

31.12. 'Be grateful to God: he who is grateful, is grateful only for the good of his own soul. But if anyone is ungrateful, then surely God is self-sufficient and praiseworthy.'

31.16.....Truly, God is the knower of all subtleties and He is aware.

31.22. He who submits himself completely to God, and is a doer of good, has surely grasped a strong handle, for the final outcome of all events rests with God.

31.23.....for God knows well all that is in the human hearts.

31.26. Whatever is in the heavens and the earth belongs to God. Assuredly, God is self sufficient and praiseworthy.

31. 27. If all the trees on earth were pens, and the sea [were] ink, with seven [more] seas added to it, the words of God would not be exhausted: for, truly, God is Almighty and Wise.

31.28. Creating and resurrecting all of you is just like creating and resurrecting a single soul. Truly, God hears all and observes all.

31.29. God is well aware of what you do?

31.30.....God is the Most High, the Supreme One.

31.34......Surely, God is all knowing, all-aware.

Prostration (Al-Sajdah)

32.2. This Book has beyond all doubt been revealed by the Lord of the Universe.

32.3......It is the truth from your Lord to warn a people to whom, before

you, no warner came, so that hopefully they may be rightly guided.

32.6. Such is the Knower of the unseen and the visible, the Powerful, the

Merciful, 32.7. who gave everything its perfect form.

32.30. So turn away from them and wait.

The Confederates (Al-Ahzab)

33.1.......God is all-knowing and all-wise.

33.2. Follow what is revealed to you from your Lord. God is aware of all that you do.

33.3. Put your trust in God; God is sufficient as a Guardian.

33.5..... You will not be blamed if you make a mistake, you will be held accountable only for what in your hearts you have done intentionally. God is forgiving and merciful.

33.21. You have indeed in the Prophet of God a good example for those of you who look to God and the Last Day, and remember God always.

33.25....God is strong and all-powerful.

33.29.....that God has prepared a great reward for those of you who do good deeds.

33.35.....men and women who are ever mindful of God—God is ready with forgiveness and an immense reward.

33.37....The commandment of God must be fulfilled.

33.39. Those who conveyed God's messages and feared Him, and feared none but God: God suffices as a Reckoner.

33.41. Believers, remember God often.

33.42. Glorify Him morning and evening.

33.43. It is He who sends blessings to you, as do His angels, so that He may bring you out of the darkness into the light. He is most merciful to the believers.

33.44. On the Day they meet Him, they will be welcomed with the greeting, 'Peace!' He has prepared an honorable reward for them.

33.45. O Prophet, We have sent forth you as a witness, as a bearer of good news and a warner.

33.46. As one who calls people to God by His leave, and guides them like a shining light.

33.47. Convey to the believers the good news that God has bounteous blessings in store for them.

33.48. Do not yield to those who deny the truth and the hypocrites: ignore their hurtful talk. Put your trust in God; God is your all sufficient guardian.

33.51. God knows what is in your hearts; and God is all knowing, and forbearing.

33.52......God is watchful over all things.

33.54. Whether you reveal anything or hide it, God is aware of everything.

33.62....You shall find no change in the ways of God.

33.70. Believers, fear God and say the right word.

33.71. He will bless your works for you and forgive you your sins. Whoever obeys God and His Messenger has indeed achieved a great success

33.73.......but God will turn in His mercy to believing men and believing women; God is most forgiving and most merciful.

Sheba (Saba')

34.1. Praise be to God, to whom belongs all that the heavens and the earth contain and praise be to Him in the Hereafter. He is the All Wise, the All Aware.

34.2. He knows whatever goes into the earth and whatever comes forth from it, and whatever descends from heaven and whatever ascends into it. He is the Merciful, the Forgiving.

34.3.....WHO knows the unseen. Not the smallest particle in the heavens or the earth, or anything less or greater than that escapes Him; all is recorded in an open Book.

34.4. HE will surely reward those who believe and do good deeds: they shall have forgiveness and an honorable provision.

34.6. Those who have been given knowledge know that what has been revealed to you from your Lord is the truth, and that it guides to the path of the Almighty, the Praiseworthy.

34.20.....Your Lord is watchful over all things.

34.23..... HE is the Most High, the Supreme One.

34.26...'Our Lord will gather us together; then He will judge between us with truth and justice. He is the Just Decider, the All Knowing.

34.27........For He alone is God, the Mighty One, the Wise One.'

34.28. We have sent you as a bearer of glad tidings and a warner for the whole of mankind,

34.37....It is those who believe and act righteously who will be doubly rewarded for their good deeds, and will dwell in peace in the high pavilions [of paradise],

34.39....It is my Lord who increases the provision for such of His servants as He pleases, and decreases it for such of them as He pleases. Whatever you spend, He will recompense you for it. He is the best of providers.'

34.47......It is God alone who will reward me: He is the witness of all things.'

34.48. Say to them, 'My Lord hurls forth the Truth [at falsehood] and He is the knower of hidden things.'

34.49. Say to them, 'The Truth has come and will endure. Falsehood has no power to originate any good, nor to reproduce it.'

The Creator (Fatir)

35.1. All praise be to God, Creator of the heavens and the earth, who made the angels His messengers, with wings—two, or three, or four pairs. He adds to His creation whatever He wills; for God has the power to will anything.

35.2. No one can withhold the blessings God bestows upon people, nor can anyone apart from Him bestow whatever He withholds: He is the Almighty, the Wise One.

35.3. People, remember God's favour to you. Is there any creator other than God who provides for you from the heavens and the earth? There is no God save Him. How then are you turned away from the truth.

35.4.....To God all affairs will be returned.

35.5. O Men. The promise of God is true. Let not the life of this world deceive you, nor let the Deceiver deceive you about God.

35.10. If anyone seeks glory, let him know that glory belongs to God alone. Good words ascend to Him and righteous deeds are exalted by Him.

35.11...no female conceives or gives birth without His knowledge; and no one's life is prolonged or shortened, but it is recorded in a Book. That surely is easy for God.

35.13....Such is God, your Lord: His is the kingdom.

35.14....No one can tell you [the Truth] like the One who is all knowing.

35.15. O men! It is you who stand in need of God—God is self sufficient, and praiseworthy—

35.16. if He so wished, He could take you away and replace you with a

new creation; 35.17. that is not difficult for God.

35.18. No burden bearer shall bear another's burden,....... You can only warn those who fear their Lord in the unseen, and pray regularly.

Anyone who purifies himself will benefit greatly from doing so. To God all shall return.

35.23. You are but a warner—35.24.We have sent you with the truth as a bearer of good news and a warner.

35.29. Those who read the Book of God and attend to their prayers and spend in charity in private and in public out of what We have provided them, may hope for a commerce that suffers no loss.

35.30. He will give them their full rewards and give them more out of His bounty. He is forgiving and appreciative.

35.31. The Book which We have revealed to you is the truth confirming previous scriptures. God knows and observes His servants.

35.32. We have bestowed the Book on those of Our servants whom We have chosen...... some, by God's leave, excel others in good deeds. This is a great bounty of God: 35.33. they shall enter the Gardens of Eternity,

35.34......Our Lord is forgiving and appreciative.

35.38. God knows the hidden reality of the heavens and the earth. He has full knowledge of what is in the hearts of men;

35.39. It is He who has made you inherit the earth.

35.43.....You will never find any change in the ways of God; nor will you ever find God's decree averted.

35.44.....Nothing in the heavens or the earth can ever frustrate God's [plans]. He is all knowing and all powerful.

35.45. If God were to take men to task for their misdeeds, He would not leave a single living creature on the surface of the earth; but He grants them respite until an appointed time; and when their appointed time comes, then they will know that God is indeed observant of all His servants.

Ya Sin (Ya Sin)

36.2. By the Quran, full of wisdom, 36.3. you are indeed one of the messengers 36.4. on a straight path, 36.5. with a revelation sent down by the Mighty One, the Merciful, 35.6. so that you may warn a people,

36.11. You can warn only those who would follow the Reminder and fear the Gracious God, unseen. Give them the good news of forgiveness and a noble reward.

36.12. We shall surely bring the dead back to life and We record what they send ahead and what they leave behind. We have recorded everything in a clear book.

36.81. He is indeed the Supreme Creator, the All Knowing:

36.82. when He decrees a thing, He need only say, 'Be!' and it is.

36.83. So glory be to Him who has control over all things. It is to Him that you will all be brought back.

The Ranks (Al-Saffat)

37.4. Your God is One, 37.5. Lord of the heavens and the earth and everything between them.

37.40. But the chosen servants of God; 37.41. shall have a known provision—37.42. fruits of various kinds; and they shall be honored, 37.43. in the Gardens of Bliss,

37.159. God is far above what they attribute to Him.

37.180. Glory be to your Lord: the Lord of Glory is far above what they attribute to Him. 37.181. Peace be upon the Messengers 37.182. and praise be to God, the Lord of all the Worlds.

SAD (SAD)

38.29. This is a blessed Book which We sent down to you [Muhammad], for people to ponder over its messages, and for those with understanding to take heed.

38.49. This is a Reminder. The righteous shall have a good place to return to: 38.50. the Gardens of eternity with gates thrown wide open to them. 38.51. They will be comfortably seated; reclining, they will call for abundant fruit and drink; 38.52. with them, they will have pure, modest women of an equal age. 38.53. This is what you were promised on the Day of Reckoning: 38.54. Our provision for you will never be exhausted.

38.65. Say, [Prophet], 'I am only a warner. There is no god but God, the One, the All-Powerful, 38.66. Lord of the heavens and earth and everything between them, the Almighty, the Most Forgiving.'

38.86. Say, 'I do not ask you for any recompense for this, nor am I a man of false pretentions: 38.87. this is simply an admonition to mankind, 38.88. you shall before long know its truth.'

The Crowds (Al-Zumar)

39.1. This Book is sent down by God the Mighty, the Wise. 39.2. It is We who sent down the Book to you [Prophet] with the Truth, so worship God with your total devotion: 39.3. it is to God alone that sincere obedience is due.

39.4......but Glory be to Him! [He is above such things.] He is God, the One, the Omnipotent.

39.5. He created the heavens and the earth for a true purpose.

39.6......Such is God, your Lord. Sovereignty is His. There is no god but Him. So what has made you turn away?

39.7. If you are ungrateful, remember that God has no need of you. He is not pleased by ingratitude in His servants; if you are grateful, He is pleased [to see] it in you. No soul shall bear another's burden. You will

return to your Lord in the end and He will declare to you what you have done: He knows well what is in the hearts of men.

39.10. Say, '[God says] O My servants who have believed, fear your Lord. For those who do good in this world will have a good reward—and God's earth is spacious. Truly, those who persevere patiently will be

requited without measure.'

39.11. Say, 'I have been commanded to serve God, dedicating my worship entirely to Him. 39.12. I have been commanded to be the first to submit.'

39.14. Say, 'It is God I serve, sincere in my faith in Him alone.

39.17. There is good news for those who shun the worship of false deities and turn to God, so give good news to My servants, 39.18. who listen to what is said and follow what is best in it. These are the ones God has guided; these are the people endowed with understanding.

39.20. This is God's promise: God never fails in His promise.

39.23. God has sent down the best Message: a Scripture that is consimilar and oft-repeated: that causes the skins of those in awe of their Lord to creep. Then their skins and their hearts soften at the mention of God: such is God's guidance. He bestows it upon whoever He will; but no one can guide those whom God leaves to stray.

39.28. a Quran in Arabic, free from any ambiguity—so that people may be mindful.

39.33. He who brings the truth, and he who testifies to it as such—those are surely the people who are God fearing: 39.34. they will have everything they wish for from their Lord. Such is the reward of those who do good:

39.36. Is God not enough for His servant?

39.37. but he whom God guides cannot be led astray by anyone Is God not mighty and capable of retribution?

39.38......Say, 'God is sufficient for me. In Him let the faithful put their trust.'

39.41. [O Prophet!] We have sent down to you the Book for mankind with the truth. Then whoever adopts the right way, will do so for his own soul, and whoever goes astray, injures his own soul. You are not their custodian.

39.53. Say, [God says] 'O My servants, who have committed excesses against their own souls, do not despair of God's mercy, for God surely forgives all sins. He is truly the Most Forgiving, the Most Merciful.

39.54. Turn to your Lord and submit to Him before His scourge overtakes you, for then you shall not be helped.

39.55. Follow the best aspect of what is sent down to you from your Lord, before the scourge comes upon you unawares,

39.62. God is the Creator of all things, He has charge of everything; 39.63. the keys of the heavens and the earth belong to Him.

39.66. Therefore, you should worship God alone and be among the thankful.

39.75. 'Praise be to God, Lord of the Universe!'

The Forgiver (Ghafir)

40.2. This Book is revealed by God, the Almighty, the All Knowing. 40.3. The Forgiver of sin and the Accepter of repentance, who is severe in punishment and Infinite in His Bounty. There is no God but Him. All shall return to Him.

40.7. Those who bear the Throne, and those who are around it, glorify their Lord with His praise, and believe in Him. They ask forgiveness for those who believe, saying, 'Our Lord, You embrace all things in mercy and knowledge. Forgive those who turn to You and follow Your path. Save them from the punishment of Hell 40.8. and admit them, Lord, to the Eternal Garden You have promised to them, together with their righteous ancestors, spouses, and offspring: You alone are the Almighty; the All Wise. 40.9. Protect them from all evil deeds: those You protect from [the punishment for] evil deeds will receive Your mercy—that is the supreme success.'

40.12. Judgement rests with God, the Most High, the Most Great.

40.13. It is He who shows you His signs, and sends down provision for you from heaven; but none pays heed except the repentant.

40.14. Therefore call upon God, making faith pure for Him,

40.15. Exalted and throned on high, He lets the Spirit descend at His behest upon whichever of His servants He will, so that he may warn of the Day of Meeting, 40.16. the Day when they shall rise up [from their graves] and nothing about them will be hidden from God. 'To whom shall the kingdom belong that Day?' It shall belong to God, the One, the All Powerful. 40.17. That Day every soul shall be requited for what it has earned. On that Day none shall be wronged. And God is swift in reckoning.

40.19. [for] He is aware of the [most] stealthy glance, and of all that the hearts conceal.

40.20. God will judge with [justice and] truth: but those whom they invoke besides Him, have no power to judge at all. Surely, God is all hearing, all seeing.

40.39. O my people, the life of this world is only a temporary provision; and the Hereafter is the permanent abode.

40.40.....but whoever does good, whether male or female, and is a believer, will enter the Garden; where they will be provided for without Measure.

40.44....I shall entrust my affair to God, for God is observant of all [His] servants.'

40.55. So be patient, for what God has promised is sure to come. Ask forgiveness for your sins; praise your Lord morning and evening.

40.56. Seek refuge in God, for He is the All Hearing, the All Seeing.

40.57. Certainly, the creation of the heavens and the earth is greater than the creation of mankind; but most people do not know this.

40.59. The Final Hour is sure to come, without doubt, but most people do not believe.

40.60. Your Lord has said, 'Call on Me, and I will answer your prayers.

40.62. Such is God, your Lord, the Creator of all things. There is no god but He. How then are you being turned away [from Him]?

40.64. It is God who has given you the earth for a resting place and the heavens for a canopy. He shaped you, formed you well, and provided you with good things. Such is God, your Lord, so glory be to Him, the Lord of the Universe.

40.65. He is the Living One. There is no deity save Him. So pray to Him, making religion pure for Him [only]. Praise be to God, the Lord of the Universe!

40.68. It is He who gives life and death, and when He ordains a thing, He says only, 'Be!' and it is.

40.77. So be patient [O, Prophet], for God's promise is true:

40.8. He shows you His signs; which then of the signs of God will you deny?

Revelations Well Expounded (Fussilat)

41.2. A revelation from [God], the Most Gracious, the Most Merciful, 41.3. a Book whose revelations are well expounded, an Arabic Quran for people who possess knowledge, 4 proclaiming good news and a warning. Yet most of them turn away and so do not listen.

41.6. Say, 'I am only a human being like yourselves. It has been revealed to me that your God is One God. So take the straight path to Him and ask His forgiveness.'

41.8. 'The ones who believe and perform good deeds shall have a reward which will never be withheld from them.

41.9....... He is the Lord of the Universe....

41.30. As for those who affirm, 'Our Lord is God,' and then remain steadfast, the angels will descend on them, saying, 'Have no fear and do not grieve. Rejoice in the [good news of the] Garden that you have been promised. 41.31. 'We are your companions in this life and in the Hereafter. Therein you shall have all that your souls desire, and therein you shall have all that you ask for 41.32. as a rich provision from One who is ever forgiving and most merciful.'

41.33. Who speaks better than one who calls to God and does good works and says, 'I am surely of those who submit'?

41.34. Good and evil deeds are not equal. Repel evil with what is better; then you will see that one who was once your enemy has become your dearest friend,

41.35. but no one will be granted such goodness except those who exercise patience and self-restraint—no one is granted it save those who are truly fortunate.

41.36. If a prompting from Satan should stir you, seek refuge with God: He is the All Hearing and the All Knowing.

41.37. Among His signs are the night and the day, and the sun and the moon. Do not prostrate yourselves before the sun and the moon, but prostrate yourselves before God who created them all, if it is truly Him that you worship.

41.39....surely He has power over all things.

41.40.....Do as you will He sees whatever you do.

41.41. Those who reject the Reminder [the Quran] when it comes to them [are the losers] — truly it is a mighty Book: It is a revelation from the Wise, the One worthy of all praise.

41.43. Nothing is said to you but what was said indeed to the messengers before you; surely your Lord is the Lord of forgiveness...

41.46. Whoever does what is just and right, does so for his own good; and whoever does evil, does so to his own detriment: and God is never in the least unjust to His creatures.

41.47. He alone has knowledge of the Hour [of Judgment].

41.53. We shall show them Our signs in the universe and within themselves, until it becomes clear to them that this is the Truth. Is it not enough that your Lord is the witness of all things? 41.54. Yet they still doubt that they will ever meet their Lord. Surely, He encompasses all things.

Mutual Consultation (Al-Shura)

42.3. Thus God, the Powerful, the Wise, sends revelation to you as He did to those before you.

42.4. All that is in the heavens and earth belongs to Him: He is the Exalted, the Almighty.

42.5. The heavens are almost split asunder from above as the angels sing their Lord's praise and seek forgiveness for those on earth. God is indeed the Most Forgiving, the Most Merciful.

42.6. And [as for] those who take protectors besides Him, God is watching them and you are not a guardian over them.

42.10..... [Say, therefore], 'Such is God, my Lord: in Him I have placed my trust, and to Him I always turn.'

42.11. Creator of the Heavens and the Earth, He has made spouses for you from among yourselves, as well as pairs of livestock by means of which He multiplies His creatures. Nothing can be compared with Him! He is the All Hearing, the All Seeing.

42.12. To Him belong the keys of the heavens and the earth;

42.15.....but say, 'I believe in the Book which God has sent down, and I am commanded to do justice between you: God is our Lord and your Lord; we are responsible for what we do and you are responsible for what you do. There is no contention between us and you. God will gather us together, for to Him we shall return.'

42.17. It is God who has sent down the Book with the truth and the scales of justice. What will make you realize that the Hour might well have drawn near?

42.19. God is most Gracious to His creatures: He provides sustenance for whoever He wills—for He alone is the Powerful One, the Almighty.

42.22....Whereas, those who have believed and done righteous deeds, will be in the meadows of the Garden and shall have whatever they desire from their Lord. That will be the supreme favour.

42.23. These are the glad tidings which God gives to His servants who believe and do righteous deeds...... Whoever earns a good deed, We shall increase its good for him God is most forgiving, most appreciative.

42.24.....If God so willed, He could seal your heart. God wipes out falsehood and vindicates the truth by His words. He has full knowledge of what is in men's hearts—

42.25. He accepts repentance from His servants and pardons their sins. He knows everything you do.

42.26. He responds to those who believe and do good deeds, and gives them more of His bounty; agonizing torment awaits the deniers of the truth.

42.27....but He sends down in due measure whatever He will, for He is well aware of His servants and watchful over them:

42.28....He is the Protector, Worthy of All Praise.

42.30. Whatever misfortune befalls you is of your own doing—God forgives much—

42.31. ...You have no protector or helper other than God.

42.36. Whatever you have been given is only a temporary provision of this life, but that which is with God is better and more lasting for those who believe and put their trust in their Lord;

42.43 whoever is patient and forgiving, acts with great courage and resolution.

42.48. Now if they turn away, We have not sent you [O Prophet] as their keeper: your responsibility is only to convey the message.

42.49. God has control of the heavens and the earth; He creates whatever He will—

42.51. Truly, He is exalted and wise.

42.52.....You are indeed guiding to the straight path, 42.53. the path of God, to whom belongs all that is in the heavens and on the earth. Indeed all matters return eventually to God.

Ornaments of Gold (Al-Zukhruf)

43.2. By the Book that makes things clear, 43.3.We have made it an Arabic Quran so that you may understand. 43.4. Truly, it is inscribed in the Original Book, in Our keeping; it is sublime and full of wisdom.

43.14. And to our Lord we shall surely return.'

43.32....It is We who distribute among them their livelihood in the life of this world, and raise some of them above others in rank, so that they may take one another into service; and the mercy of your Lord is better than [the wealth] which they amass.

43.43. So, hold fast to the Book that has been revealed to you—you are surely on the right path—

43.44. it is certainly a reminder to you and to your people and you will soon be called to account.

43.64. For God, He is my Lord and your Lord: so worship Him: that is a straight path.

43.68. 'O My servants, you need not fear this Day, nor shall you grieve'—

43.82. But—exalted be the Lord of the heavens and earth, the Lord of the Throne— He is far above their [false] descriptions.

43.84. It is He who is God in heaven, and God on earth: He is the Wise One, the All Knowing;

43.85. blessed be He who has sovereignty over the kingdom of the heavens and the earth and all that lies between them. He alone has knowledge of the Hour, and to Him you shall be returned.

Smoke (Al-Dukhan)

44.2. By the Book that makes things clear, 44.3. surely We sent it down on a blessed night—We have always sent warnings—44.4. on that night every wise decree is specified 44.5. by Our own command—We have been sending messages, 44.6. as a mercy from your Lord, He hears all and knows all, 44.7. He is the Lord of heaven and earth and all that is between them—if only you would really believe—44.8. there is no deity save Him: It is He who gives both life and death—He is your Lord, and the Lord of your forefathers,

44.38. We did not idly create the heavens and the earth and all that lies between them; 44.39. We did not create them save with a purpose, yet most people have no knowledge of this.

44.40. Truly, the Day of Decision is the appointed time for all of them.

44.41.......Surely, He is the Mighty, the Merciful One.

44.58. We have made this Quran easy to understand—in your own language—so that they may take heed.

Kneeling (Al-Jathiyah)

45.2. This Scripture is sent down from God, the Mighty and Wise One.

45.3. There are signs in the heavens and the earth for those who believe:

45.6. These are God's revelations, which We recite to you in all truth.

45.13. He has subjected whatever is in heaven and on the earth to you; it is all from Him. In that are signs for those who ponder.

45.15. Whoever does what is just and right, does so for his own good; and whoever does evil, does so to his own detriment, and you shall all return to your Lord.

45.18. Then We set you on a clear path [of religion]: so follow it, and do not yield to the desires of those who have no knowledge.

45.19....while the friend of the righteous is God.

45.20. This [Book] brings enlightenment and guidance to mankind, and is a blessing for those who have firm faith.

45.22. God has created the heavens and the earth for a true purpose, so that every soul may be rewarded for whatever it has earned, and no one will be wronged.

45.26. Say, 'God gives you life, then causes you to die, and then will gather you together for the Day of Resurrection, about which there is no doubt. But most people do not know it.'

45.27. To God belongs the kingdom of the heavens and the earth; on the Day when the Hour comes.

45.30. Those who believed and did good deeds will be admitted by their Lord into His mercy—that shall be the manifest triumph.

45.36 Praise, then, be to God, Lord of the heavens, and Lord of the earth, the Lord of all the worlds.

45.37. All greatness belongs to Him in the heavens and earth. He is the Almighty, the All Wise.

The Sand Dunes (Al-Ahqaf)

46.2. This Book is sent down from God, the Almighty, the Wise One. 46.3. We created the heavens and the earth and all that lies between them purely for just ends, and for a specific term....

46.13. Surely those who say, 'Our Lord is God,' and remain firm [on that path] shall feel no fear, nor shall they grieve: 46.14. it is they who are the people of Paradise, they shall abide therein as a reward for all that they have done.

46.16. We accept from such people the best of what they do and We overlook their bad deeds. They will be among the people of Paradise—this is a true promise that has been given to them.

46.19. All will be ranked according to their deeds. We will requite them in full for their actions and they will not be wronged.

46.31. Our people, respond to the one who calls you to God. Believe in him! God will forgive you your sins and protect you.......

46.32. But he who does not respond to God's calls can never elude [Him] on earth, nor can he have any protector against Him.

46.33. Have they not seen that God, who created the heavens and the earth and was not wearied by their creation, has the power to bring the dead back to life? Yes, indeed, He has power over all things.

46.35. Have patience,......

Muhammad (Muhammad)

47.2. As for those who believe and do good deeds and believe in what has been revealed to Muhammad—and it is the truth from their Lord—God will remove their sins from them and set their condition right.

47.7. Believers! If you succour God, He will succour you and make your footsteps firm.

47.11. .... God is the protector of the believers......

47.17. But as for those who follow guidance, He adds to their guidance, and shows them the way to righteousness.

47.19. Know then that there is no god except God. Ask forgiveness for your wrongdoing and for the men and women who believe. God knows both your movements and your lodging.

47.30.....God knows all that you do.

47.31. Most certainly We will try you until We have discovered those among you who strive their hardest, and those who are steadfast, and will test your record.

47.33. Believers, obey God and obey the Messenger: do not let your deeds go to waste-

47.35. So do not lose heart or appeal for peace when you have gained the upper hand. God is with you and will never let your works go to waste.

47.36. The life of this world is only a game, a pastime, but if you believe and are mindful of God, He will recompense you and will not ask you for your wealth.

47.38. Behold! You are those who are called upon to spend for God's cause, but among you are those who are niggardly, and whoever stints does so against his own self. Indeed, God is self sufficient, but you stand in need [of Him], and if you turn back, He will bring in your place another people, who will not be like you.

Victory (Al-Fath)

48.1. Truly, We have granted you a clear victory 48.2. so that God may

forgive you your past and future sins and complete His favour to you and guide you to a straight path, 48.3. and so that God might bestow on you His mighty help.

48.4. It was He who sent down tranquility into the hearts of the believers, to add faith to their faith—the forces of the heavens and earth belong to Him; He is all knowing and all wise—48.5. and so that He might admit the believers, men and women, into Gardens through which rivers flow, to dwell therein forever, and so that He may remove their evils from the —that is, indeed, a supreme triumph in God's eyes—

48.7. The forces of heavens and earth belong to God; He is almighty and all wise.

48.8. We have sent you [Muhammad] forth as a witness and a bearer of good tidings and a warner, 48.9. so that you may believe in God and His Messenger, and may help him, and honor him, and so that you may glorify God morning and evening.

48.10. Behold, all who pledge their allegiance to you[Muhammad] indeed pledge their allegiance to God: the hand of God is over their hands. Hence, he who breaks his oath breaks it only to his own loss. Whereas he who remains true to what he has pledged to God, shall have a great reward bestowed upon him by God.

48.11.....Say, 'Who then has any power at all [to intervene] on your behalf with God, if His will is to do you harm, or if He intends to do you good? Indeed, God is well aware of all that you do.'

48.14. To God belongs the kingdom of the heavens and the earth. He forgives whom He pleases, and punishes whom He pleases. And God is most forgiving and merciful.

48.17......God will admit anyone who obeys Him and His Messenger to Gardens through which rivers flow.

48.20. God has promised you many future gains....

48.23. such was the law of God in the past; and you shall find no change in the law of God.

48.24.....God sees what you do.

48.28. He is the One who has sent His Messenger with guidance and the true religion, so that He may have it prevail over all [other] religions. God suffices as a witness!

48.29. Muhammad is the Messenger of God.........God has promised forgiveness and a great reward to those of them who believe and do good works.

The Apartments (Al-Hujurat)

49.1.....Fear God—God hears all and knows all.

49.6. Believers, if an evil-doer brings you news, ascertain the correctness of the report fully, lest you unwittingly harm others, and then regret what you have done.

49.7.....However, God has endeared the faith to you, and beautified it in your hearts, and has made denial of the truth, wickedness, and disobedience hateful to you. People such as these are rightly guided 49.8. through God's bounty and favour; God is all knowing, and wise.

49.9.....Truly, God loves the just.

49.10. Surely all believers are brothers. So make peace between your brothers, and fear God, so that mercy may be shown to you.

49.11. Believers, let not some men among you ridicule others: it may be that the latter are better than the former: nor should some women laugh at others: it may be that the latter are better than the former: do not defame or be sarcastic to each other, or call each other by [offensive] nicknames. How bad it is to earn an evil reputation after accepting the faith!

49.12. Believers, avoid much suspicion. Indeed some suspicion is a sin. And do not spy on one another and do not backbite......Fear God, God is ever forgiving and most merciful.

49.13. Mankind! We have created you from a male and female, and made you into peoples and tribes, so that you might come to know each other. The noblest of you in God's sight is the one who fears God most. God is all knowing and all-aware.

49.14.....But if you will obey God and His Messenger, He will not detract anything from your good deeds. God is most forgiving and ever merciful.'

49.15. The believers are only those who have faith in God and His Messenger and then doubt not, but strive, hard with their wealth and their persons for the cause of God. Such are the truthful ones.

49.16.....God has knowledge of all things.

49.17......Say, 'Do not consider your Islam a favour to me. No indeed! It is God who bestowed a favour on you by guiding you to the true faith.

49.18. God knows the unseen things of the heavens and the earth. God sees all that you do.

Qaf (Qaf)

50.16. We created man—We know the promptings of his soul, and are closer to him than his jugular vein—50.17. and the two recording angels are recording, sitting on the right and the left: 50.18. each word he utters shall be noted down by a vigilant guardian. 50.19. The trance of death will come revealing the truth: that is what you were trying to escape.

50.38. We created the heavens, the earth, and everything between them in six days [periods] nor were We ever wearied.

50.39. So bear with patience what they say, and glorify your Lord with His praise, before the rising and before the setting of the sun; 50.40. proclaim His praise in the night and at the end of every prayer.

50.43. Truly, it is We who give life and cause death, and to Us shall all return.

50.45....so remind, with this Quran, those who fear My warning.

Scattering Winds (Al-Dhariyat)

51.5. What you are promised is certainly true: 51.6 the Judgement will surely come to pass.

51.20. On the earth, and in yourselves, 51.21. there are signs for firm believers. Do you not see then? 51.22. In heaven is your sustenance, and also that which you are promised. 51.23. By the Lord of the heaven and the earth, it is certainly the truth. It is as true as your ability to speak.

51.47. We built the universe with Our might, giving it its vast expanse. 51.48. We have spread out the earth—how well We have spread it out—51.49. and We created pairs of all things so that you might reflect.

51.50. Therefore hasten to God; truly, I am sent by Him to give you clear warning.

51.51. Do not set up another god, along with God. I come from Him to warn you plainly.

51.58. it is God who is the great Sustainer, the Mighty One, the Invincible.

Mount Sinai (Al-Tur)

52.17. Truly, the God-fearing will dwell [on that Day] in gardens and in bliss.

52.48. So wait patiently for the Judgement of your Lord—you are certainly under Our watchful eye. And glorify and celebrate the praises of your Lord when you rise up [from your sleep].

52.49. Extol His glory at night, and at the setting of the stars.

The Setting Star (Al-Najm)

53.4. It [Quran] is nothing but revelation sent down to him [Muhammad].

53.25 But it is to God that the Hereafter and this world belong.

53.29. So ignore those who turn away from Our revelation and seek nothing but the life of this world.

53.31. Everything in the heavens and on the earth belongs to God and so He will requite those who do evil in accordance with their deeds and will reward those left with that which is best, for those who do good. 53. 32. As for those who refrain from committing grave sins and indecent acts, though they may commit minor offences, your Lord is unstinting in His

forgiveness. He knows you when He brings you out of the earth, and when you were embryos in the wombs of your mothers; so do not make claims to be pure. He knows best who is truly righteous.

53.38. that no soul shall bear the burden of another; 53.39. and that man shall have only that for which he strives; 53.40. and that [the fruit of] his striving shall soon be seen; 53.41. and in the end he will be repaid for it in full; 53.42. that all things in the end shall return to God; 53.43. that it is He who brings laughter and tears; 53.44. that it is He who causes death and gives life; 53.45. and that He Himself created the two sexes: male and female, 53.46. from an ejected drop of sperm; 53.47. and that He will bring about the Second Creation; 53.48. that it is He who gives wealth and possessions;

53.62. Prostrate yourselves before God, and worship Him alone!

The Moon (Al-Qamar)

54.17. We have made it easy to learn lessons from the Quran. Is there anyone who would receive admonition?

54.22. We have made it easy to learn lessons from the Quran: is there anyone who would receive admonition?

54.32. Indeed, We have made the Quran easy to learn lessons from. Is there anyone who would receive admonition?

54.49. We have created everything in due measure;

54.50. We command but once: Our will is done in the twinkling of an eye;

54.54. The God conscious will find themselves in gardens and rivers, 54.55. in the seat of truth with an all-powerful sovereign.

The Merciful (Al-Rahman)

55.1. The Merciful 55.2. who taught the Quran—55.3. He created man 55.4. and He taught him speech. 55.5. The sun and the moon move according to a fixed reckoning; 55.6. the stars and the trees bend in prostration.

55.7. He raised the heavens and set up the measure, 55.8. so that you should not transgress the measure. 55.9. Always measure with justice and do not give short measure.

55.10. He has laid out the earth for His creatures. 55.11. On it are fruits and palm-trees with sheathed clusters [of dates], 55.12. and grains with their husk and fragrant plants. 55.13. Which of your Lord's wonders would you deny?

55.14. He has created man, from dry ringing clay, like the potter's, 55.15. and He created the jinns from a flame of fire. 55.16. Which of your Lord's wonders would you deny?

55.17. He is the Lord of the two easts and the Lord of the two wests. 55.18. Which of your Lord's wonders would you deny? 55.19. He has set the two oceans in motion, converging together. 55.20. Between them is a barrier, which they do not overrun. 55.21. Which of your Lord's wonders would you deny? 55.22. Pearls and corals come forth from both of them. 55.23. Which, of your Lord's wonders would you deny? 55.24. His are the lofty ships that rear aloft on the sea like mountains. 55.25. Which of your Lord's wonders would you deny?

55.26. All that is on the earth is doomed to perish, 55.27. while your Lord's own Self will remain full of majesty and glory. 55.28. Which of your Lord's wonders would you deny? 55.29. Everyone in the heavens and on the earth entreats Him. Every day He manifests Himself in a new state. 55.30. Which of your Lord's wonders would you deny?

55.31. Soon We shall attend to you—two big groups [of jinn and mankind]. 55.32. Which of your Lord's wonders would you deny?

55.33. O company of jinn and men! If you have the power to go beyond the realms of the heavens and the earth, pass beyond them: you cannot pass out but with [Our] authority. 55.34. Which of your Lord's wonders would you deny? 55.35. Flames of fire and molten brass shall be sent against both of you, and you will not be able to defend yourselves. 55.36. Which of your Lord's wonders would you deny?

55.46. There are two gardens for one who fears standing before his Lord. 55.47. Which of your Lord's wonders would you deny? 55.48. [There will be two gardens with] spreading branches. 55.49. Which of your Lord's wonders would you deny? 55.50. In both of them, there are two springs flowing. 55.51. Which of your Lord's wonders would you deny? 55.52. In both of them, there will be two kinds of every fruit. 55.53. Which of your Lord's wonders would you deny? 55.54. They will recline upon carpets lined with rich brocade; and the fruits of both these

gardens will be within easy reach. 55.55. Which of your Lord's wonders

would you deny? 55.56. Therein are maidens of modest gaze, whom neither a man nor a jinn had ever touched before them. 55.57. Which of your Lord's wonders would you deny? 55.58. [There will be] maidens as fair as corals and rubies. 55.59. Which of your Lord's wonders would you deny? 55.60. The reward of goodness shall be nothing but goodness. 55.61. Which of your Lord's wonders would you deny? 55.62. Besides those two there shall be two other gardens. 55.63. Which of your Lord's wonders would you deny? 55.64. Both [gardens] of the darkest green. 55.65. Which of your Lord's wonders would you deny? 55.66. In both of them live springs gush forth. 55.67. Which of your Lord's wonders would you deny? 55.68. In both of them there will be fruit trees and date-palms and pomegranates. 55.69. Which of your Lord's wonders would you deny? 55.70. Therein will be maidens chaste and beautiful. 55.71. Which of your Lord's wonders would you deny? 55.72. [There the blessed will live with their] pure companions sheltered in pavilions. 55.73. Which of your Lord's wonders would you deny? 55.74. Whom neither a man or jinn had ever touched before them. 55.75. Which of your Lord's wonders would you deny? 55.76. [They will live in such a paradise] reclining upon green cushions and the finest carpets. 55.77. Which of your Lord's wonders would you deny?

55.78. Blessed be your Lord's name, full of glory and majesty!

The Inevitable Event (Al-Waqi‘Ah)

56.1 When the inevitable event takes place, 56.2. and there can be no denying its happening, 56.3. some shall be abased and others exalted.

56.57. We have created you: why then do you not accept the truth?

56.96. So glorify the name of your Lord, the Supreme.

Iron (Al-Hadid)

57.1. Everything in the heavens and earth glorifies God—He is the Mighty, the Wise One.

57.2. He has sovereign control over the heavens and the earth. He gives life and brings death. He has power over all things.

57.3. He is the First and the Last, the Outward and the Inward. He has knowledge of all things.

57.4. He is with you wherever you are; He sees all that you do;

57.5. He has sovereignty over the heavens and the earth. All affairs will return to God.

57.6. And He knows all that is in the hearts of men.

57.7. Have faith in God and His Messenger and spend in charity from that of which He has made you trustees: those of you who believe and give alms shall be richly rewarded.

57.9. God is indeed compassionate and merciful to you.

57.10......Yet God has promised you all a good reward. He is aware of all that you do.

57.11. Who will offer God a generous loan? He will double it for him and give him a rich reward.

57.16. Has the time not come for the faithful when their hearts in all humility should engage in the remembrance of God and of the revelation of truth,

57.16. Has the time not come for the faithful when their hearts in all humility should engage in the remembrance of God and of the revelation of truth,

57.17. Remember that God brings the earth back to life after its death. We have made Our signs clear to you, so that you may fully understand.

57.18. Alms-givers, both men and women, who give a generous loan to God, shall have it multiplied and shall have an honorable reward.

57.19. Those who believe in God and His messengers are the truthful ones and the witnesses in the sight of their Lord. They shall have their reward and their light.

57.20. Never forget that the life of this world is only a game and a passing delight, a show, and mutual boasting and trying to outrival each other in riches and children.......the life of this world is nothing but means of deception.

57.21. Vie with one another for your Lord's forgiveness and for a Paradise as vast as heaven and earth, which has been made ready for those who believe in God and His messengers. Such is God's grace. He bestows it upon whoever He pleases. There is no limit to God's bounty.

57.22. No misfortune can affect the earth or your own selves without its first having been recorded in a book, before We bring it into being. That is easy for God to do; 57.23. so that you may not grieve for what has escaped you, nor be exultant over what you have gained. God loves neither the conceited nor the boastful, 57.24. nor those who, being miserly themselves, urge others to be miserly. He who turns his back should remember that God alone is self-sufficient and worthy of all praise.

57.25. We sent Our messengers with evidence and, with them, We sent down the Book and the Scales of Justice, so that men might act in all fairness.

57.28. Believers, fear God and believe in His messenger. He will show you mercy in double measure and will provide a light for you to walk in. God will grant you forgiveness. He is forgiving and merciful.

57.29. The People of the Book should know that they have no power whatsoever over God's grace. His grace is entirely in His hand and He bestows it upon whoever He wills. God is truly infinite in His bounty.

The Pleading (Al-Mujadalah)

58.1. God is all hearing, all seeing.

58.2. God is pardoning, forgiving.

58.3. God is fully aware of what you do,

58.6. in the end He will tell them the truth about their conduct, on the Day of Judgement. for God is a witness to all things.

58.7. Do you not see that God knows all that is in the heavens and on the earth?........ For God has full knowledge of all things.

58.9. Believers, when you confer together in private, do not confer in support of sin and transgression and disobedience to the Messenger, but confer for the promotion of virtue and righteousness. Fear God, before whom you shall all be gathered.

58.10.....Let the believers put their trust in God.

58.11. Believers, if you are told to make room for one another in your assemblies, then do so, and God will make room for you, and if you are told to rise up, do so: God will raise in rank those of you who believe and those who have been given knowledge: He is fully aware of all that you do.

58.12........know that God is Forgiving and Merciful.

58.13.......[know that] God has turned to you in His mercy; then observe your prayers and pay the prescribed alms and obey God and His Messenger. God is aware of all that you do.

58.21........ God has decreed, 'I and My messengers shall most certainly prevail.' Truly God is Powerful and Almighty.

58.22.......has engraved faith on their very hearts and has strengthened them with a spirit of His own. He will usher them into Gardens through which rivers flow where they shall dwell forever. God is well-pleased with them and they are well pleased with Him. They are God's party. God's party shall surely enter into a state of bliss.

Banishment (Al-Hashr)

59.1. Everything in the heavens and on the earth glorifies God. He is the Almighty, the All Wise.

59.6......God has power over all things

59.10......'Our Lord, forgive us and our brothers who preceded us in the faith and leave no malice in our hearts towards those who believe. Lord,

You are indeed compassionate and merciful.'

59.18. Believers! Fear God, and let every soul look to what it lays up for the future. Fear God: God is aware of what you do.

59.22. He is God: there is no deity save Him. He knows the unseen and the visible. He is the Compassionate, the Merciful. 59.23. He is God, there is no deity save Him, the Sovereign, the Most Pure, the Source of Peace, the Granter of Security, the Protector, the Mighty, the Subduer, the Supreme, Glory be to God, who is far above what they associate with Him. 59.24. He is God—the Creator, the Originator, the Giver of Form. His are the most excellent names. Everything in the heavens and earth declares His glory. He is the Mighty, the Wise One.

She Who Is Tested (Al-Mumtahanah)

60.1........I know all that you conceal and all that you reveal........

60.3. Neither your relatives nor your children will be of any help to you on the Day of Resurrection. He will judge between you, and God sees all that you do.

60.4.....'O our Lord, in You we have placed our trust and to You we turn in repentance and to You is the final return. 5 Our Lord, do not make us a prey for those who deny the truth, and forgive us our Lord. For You alone are the Mighty, the Wise One.'

60.6......God is self sufficient and worthy of all praise.

60.7. It may well be that God will create goodwill between you and those of them with whom you are now at enmity—for God is all powerful, most forgiving and merciful.

60.8. He does not forbid you to deal kindly and justly with anyone who has not fought you on account of your faith or driven you out of your homes. God loves the just.

60.10.....He judges with justice between you. God is all knowing and all wise.

60.11.......Fear God in whom you believe.

Ranks (Al-Saff)

61.1. Everything in the heavens and earth glorifies God—He is the Almighty, the Wise.

61.9. it is He who has sent His Messenger with guidance and the true religion,

61.10. Believers! Shall I guide you to a profitable course that will save you from a painful punishment? 61.11. You should believe in God and His Messenger, and strive for God's cause with your possessions and your lives. That will be better for you, if you only knew—61.12. and He will forgive you your sins and admit you into Gardens with rivers flowing under them. He will lodge you in fine dwellings in the Gardens of Eternity; that is indeed the supreme achievement. 61.13. He will give you another blessing which you desire: help from God and imminent victory. Give good tidings [O Muhammad] to believers!

61.14. Believers, be God's helpers,

The Day of Congregation (Al-Jumu'Ah)

62.1. Whatever is in the heavens and on the earth glorifies God, the Sovereign Lord, the Holy One, the Mighty, the Wise.

62.2. It is He who has raised among the unlettered people a messenger from among themselves who recites His revelations to them, and purifies them, and teaches them the Book and wisdom,

62.4. That is God's grace; He bestows it on whom He pleases; for God is limitless in His grace.

62.10. When the prayer is ended, disperse in the land and seek to obtain [something] of God's bounty; and remember God much, so that you may prosper.

62.11.......God is the most munificent Giver.

The Hypocrites (Al-Munafiqun)

63.7.....but the treasures of the heavens and the earth belong to God,

63.8....However, all honor belongs to God, and to His Messenger and those who believe [in God],

63.9 O believers! Do not let your wealth or your children distract you from remembrance of God.

63.11. But God will not grant a reprieve to a soul when its appointed time has come; God is well-aware of what you do.

Loss and Gain (Al-Taghabun)

64.1. All that is in the heavens and on the earth extols the glory of God. To Him belongs the Kingdom and to Him all praise is due. He has power over all things.

64.2. It was He who created you; and some of you are those who deny this truth, and some who believe [in it]. God sees everything you do.

64.3. He created the heavens and the earth for a purpose. He formed you and gave you the best of forms. To Him you shall all return.

64.4. He knows whatever is in the heavens and the earth. He knows all that you conceal and all that you reveal. God is aware of what is in your hearts.

64.6......God is self sufficient and worthy of all praise.

64.7....Say, 'By my Lord, most surely you will be raised up again and then you will be told of all that you have done; and that is easy enough for God.'

64.8. Believe then in God and His Messenger, and in the light which We have sent down. God is fully aware of all that you do.

64.9. When He shall gather you all for the Day of Gathering that will be

the Day of loss and gain; and whoever believes in God and does good deeds shall be forgiven their sins and admitted to Gardens through which rivers flow, where they shall dwell forever. That is the supreme triumph.

64.11. No affliction can befall man but by God's permission—He guides the hearts of those who believe in Him: God has knowledge of all things—

64.12. obey God and obey the Messenger;

64.13. God! There is no god but He, so let the faithful put their trust in Him.

64.15. Your wealth and your children are only a trial; God's reward is great: 64.16. so be mindful of God as best as you can; and listen, and obey; and spend in charity: it is for your own good. Those who guard themselves against their own greed will surely prosper:

64.17. if you give a good loan to God, He will multiply it for you and forgive you, for God is appreciative and forbearing;

64.18. God is the Knower of the unseen and the seen: He is the Almighty, the Wise One.

Divorce (Al-Talaq)

65.1....be mindful of God, your Lord.

65.2.....To one who fears God, He will grant a way out [of his difficulties],

65.3. and God will provide for him from an unexpected source; God suffices for anyone who puts his trust in Him. God will surely bring about what He decrees. He has set a measure for all things.

65.4.....God makes things easy for those who are mindful of Him.

65.5. Such is the commandment which God has revealed to you. He who fears God shall be forgiven his sins and richly rewarded.

65.7. God does not burden any person with more than He has given him. God will soon bring about ease after hardship.

65.10....So, fear God, O men of understanding, who have believed. God has sent down to you a Reminder 65.11. and a messenger who conveys to you God's clear messages, so that he might lead those, who believe and do good deeds, out of darkness into light. God will admit those who believe in Him and do good deeds into Gardens with rivers flowing through them, where they will remain forever. God has indeed made Excellent provision for them.

65.12. It is God who created the seven heavens and the same number of earths. His commandment descends among them, so that you may know that God has power over all things; and that He encompasses all things with His knowledge.

Prohibition (Al-Tahrim)

66.2. .....God is your patron. He is the All Knowing, the Wise One.

66.8. Believers, turn to God in sincere repentance. Your Lord may well forgive your bad deeds and admit you into gardens watered by running streams, on a Day when God will not abase the Prophet and those who have believed with him. Their light will shine out ahead of them and on their right, and they will say: 'Lord perfect our light for us, and forgive us; You have power over all things.'

The Kingdom (Al-Mulk)

67.1. Blessed is He in whose hand is the Kingdom: He has power over all things;

67.2. He created death and life so that He might test you, and find out which of you is best in conduct. He is the Mighty, the Most Forgiving One.

67.3. He created seven heavens one above the other in layers. You will not find any flaw in the creation of the Gracious One.

67.12. As for those who fear their Lord in the unseen will have forgiveness and a rich reward.

67.13. Whether you speak in secret or aloud, He knows what is in every heart.

67.14. How could He who created not know His own creation, when He alone is the Most Subtle in His wisdom and the All Aware?

67.15. It is He who has made the earth subservient to you, so traverse its regions and eat its provisions. To Him you shall all be resurrected.

67.19.....Surely, He observes all things.

67.20. Who is there to defend you like an army, besides the Lord of Mercy?

67.29. Say, 'He is the Most Gracious: we believe in Him and we put our trust in Him.

The Pen (Al-Qalam)

68.3. Most surely, you will have a never ending reward.

68.34. Those who are mindful of their Lord will be rewarded with gardens of bliss.

68.48. Wait patiently for your Lord's judgement;

The Inevitable Hour (Al-Haqqah)

69.40. most surely, this is the word brought by a noble messenger,

69.43. It is a revelation sent down by the Sustainer of the Universe:

69.51. It is the indubitable truth.

69.52. So glorify the name of your Lord, the Almighty.

The Ascending Stairways (Al-Ma'Arij)

70.3......He is the Lord of the Ascending Stairways, 69.4. by which the angels and the Spirit will ascend to Him in one Day which will last for fifty thousand years.

70.5. Therefore, [O believers] behave with seemly patience.

Noah (Nuh)

71.2 [Noah] said, 'My people! I am but a plain warner to you, 71.3. that you should worship God [alone] and be conscious of Him. Pay heed to me. 71.4. He will forgive your sins and will grant you respite till an appointed time. When the time appointed by God arrives, it cannot be

postponed, if you only knew.'

71.10...'Ask forgiveness of your Lord. Surely He is the most forgiving.

71. 28. Lord! Forgive me and my parents and every true believer who enters my house, forgive all the believing men and believing women;

The Jinn (Al-Jinn)

72.1......"We have heard a really wonderful recital, 72.2. which guides to the right path; so we have believed in it and we will not associate anyone with our Lord- 72.3. and exalted is the majesty of our Lord—He has taken neither a wife nor a son.

72.13....He who believes in his Lord has no fear of loss or of injustice.

72.20. Say, 'I call only upon my Lord and do not associate anyone else with Him.' 72.21. Say, 'It is not in my power to cause you either harm or good?' 72.22. Say, 'Surely no one can protect me against God, nor can I find besides Him any place of refuge. 72.23. My duty is only to convey that which I receive from Him and His messages.'

72.26. He alone has knowledge of what is hidden. He reveals this to none, 72.27. except the messenger whom He has chosen. He sends down guardians who walk before them and behind them, 72.28. so that He may know that the messengers have delivered the messages of their Lord. He encompasses all that is with them and He keeps count of all things.

The Wrapped One (Al-Muzzammil)

73.8. Remember the name of your Lord, and devote yourself to Him wholeheartedly.

73.9. He is the Lord of the east and the west there is no deity but Him, so take Him as your Guardian.

73.20.....and give to God a goodly loan. For whatever good deed you send on before you for your souls, you will find it with God. It will be improved and richly rewarded by Him. Seek God's forgiveness, He is most forgiving, most merciful.

Wrapped In His Cloak (Al-Muddaththir)

74.3. Proclaim the glory of your Lord; 74.4 purify your garments; 74.5. shun uncleanness; 74.6. do not bestow a favour in the expectation of receiving more in return; 74.7. and for the sake of your Lord, be patient.

74.52. Indeed, everyone of them desires to have sheets of revelations unfolded before them.

74.54. but this is truly a reminder.

74.56.....He is the Lord who is worthy to be feared: the Lord of forgiveness.

The Day of Resurrection (Al-Qiyamah)

75.1. By the Day of Resurrection, 75.2. and by the self-reproaching soul! 75.3. Does man think that We cannot [resurrect him and] bring his bones together again? 75.4. Indeed, We have the power to restore his very finger tips! 75.5.Yet man wants to deny what is ahead of him:

75.12. on that Day, to your Lord alone is the recourse. 75.13. On that Day, man will be told of all that he has sent before and what he has left

behind. 75.14. Indeed, man shall be a witness against himself, 75.15. in spite of all the excuses he may offer.

75.20. Truly, you love immediate gain 75.21. and neglect the Hereafter.

75.22. Some faces will be radiant on that Day, 75.23. looking towards their Lord;

Human (Al-Insan)

76.1. Was there not a period of time when man was nothing worth mentioning? 76.2.We created man from a drop of mingled fluid so that We might try him; We gave him hearing and sight; 76.3.We showed him the way, whether he be grateful or ungrateful.

76.11. Therefore, God will ward off from them the woes of that Day, and make them find brightness and joy, 76.12. and their reward for being patient will be a Garden and silk [clothing]. 76.13. Reclining upon couches, they will find therein neither the heat of the sun nor bitter, biting cold, 76.14. the shading branches of trees will come down low over them, and their clusters of fruit, will hang down where they are the easiest to reach. 76.15. Vessels of silver and goblets of pure crystal will be passed round among them 76.16. and gleaming silver goblets which have been filled to the exact measure, 76.17. and they will be given a cup to drink flavored with ginger, 76.18. from a flowing spring called Salsabil. 76.19. They will be attended by youths who will not age—when you see them you will think them to be like sprinkled pearls 76.20. wherever you look, you will see bliss and a great kingdom: 76.21. they will wear green garments of fine silk and rich brocade. They will be adorned with silver bracelets. And their Lord will give them a pure drink. 76.22. This is your reward. Your endeavor is fully acknowledged.

76.23 .Truly, it is We who have revealed to you the Quran, a gradual revelation. 76.24. So wait patiently for the command of your Lord,

76.29. This is a reminder. Let whoever wishes, take the right path to his Lord. 76.30. But you cannot will it unless God wills [to show you that way]—God is indeed all knowing and wise.

Those That Are Sent Forth (Al-Mursalat)

77.7. that which you have been promised shall be fulfilled.

77.41. The righteous shall dwell amidst cool shades and fountains 77.42. and shall have fruits such as they desire; 77.43. [They will be told], 'Eat and drink with relish in return for what you did [in life]:77.44. this is how We reward those who do good.'

The Tidings (Al-Naba')

78.1. What are they asking each other about? 78.2. About the awesome tidings [of resurrection]

78.17. Surely, the Day of Judgement has an appointed time.

78.29. but We have recorded everything in a Book.

78.31. As for those who are mindful of God, they shall surely triumph: 78.32. theirs shall be gardens and vineyards, 78.33. and young maidens of equal age, 78.34. and overflowing cups. 78.35. There they shall not hear any idle talk, or any untruth: 78.36 all this will be a recompense, a gift, that will suffice them, from your Lord, 78.37. the Sustainer of the heavens and the earth and all that lies between them, the most Gracious-

78.39. That Day is sure to come, so whoever wishes to, let him take the path that leads towards his Lord.

The Pluckers (Al-Nazi'At)

He Frowned ('Abasa)

80.11 Indeed, this [Quran] is an admonition. 80.12. Let him who will, pay heed to it. 80.13. It is set down on honored pages, 80.14. exalted and purified, 80.15. by the hands of scribes, 80.16. exalted and purified.

Folding Up (Al-Takwir)

81.19. Truly, this is the word brought by a noble messenger, 81.20. endowed with power and held in honor by the Lord of the Throne.81.21. who is obeyed there and is worthy of trust.

81.27. This is merely a reminder to all mankind; 81.28. to every one of you who wishes to tread the straight path. 81.29. But you cannot will it unless God, the Lord of the Universe, so wills it [to show you that way].

The Cleaving Asunder (Al-Infitar)

82.6. O man! What is it that lures you away from your bountiful Sustainer, 82.7. who created you, fashioned you and proportioned you, 82.8. in whatever form He pleased?

82.10. Surely, there are guardians watching over you, 80.11. noble recorders, 82,12. who know all that you do:

82.13. the virtuous will dwell in bliss,

82.18.....what will make you realize what the Day of Judgement will be? 82.19. It will be a Day when no human being shall be of the least avail to any other human being, God [alone] will hold command on that Day.

Those Who Give Short Measure (Al-Mutaffifin)
The Bursting Open (Al-Inshiqaq)

84.1. When the sky bursts open, 84.2. and obeys its Lord as it must, 84.3. when the earth flattens out, 84.4. and casts out all that is within it and becomes empty; 84.5. and obeys its Lord as it must, 84.6. O man, having striven hard towards your Lord, you shall meet Him:

84.19. you will progress from stage to stage.

84.23. God is quite aware of what they are storing in their hearts.

84.25. But for those who believe and do good works; for them there shall be a never ending reward.

The Constellations (Al-Buruj)

85.9. to whom belongs the kingdom of the heavens and the earth. God is witness over all things.

85.11. But those who believe and do good deeds shall be rewarded with gardens watered by flowing rivers. That is the supreme triumph.

85.12. The grip of your Lord is indeed severe—

85.13. it is He who begins and repeats [His creation]—

85.14. and He is the Forgiving and Loving One. 85.15. The Lord of the

Glorious Throne, 85.16. Executor of His own will.

85.20. God encompasses them from all sides. 85.21. It is indeed a glorious Quran, 85.22. written on a preserved Tablet.

That Which Comes In the Night (Al-Tariq)

86.4. [for] no human being has been left unguarded.

86.5. Let man reflect on what he was created from.

86.17. so bear with those who deny the truth, and let them be for a little while.

The Most High (Al-A'La)

87.1. Glorify the name of your Lord, the Most High, 87.2. who created all things and gave them due proportions, 87.3. who determines the nature [of all that exists], and guided it accordingly;

87.6. [O Prophet!] We shall make you recite the Quran so that you will

not forget any of it—87.7. except whatever God wills; He knows both what is manifest and what is hidden—87.8. We shall facilitate for you the Easy Way. 87.9. Remind, if the reminder can be of benefit.

87.10 He who fears [God] will heed the reminder.

87.14. He who purifies himself, 87.15. who remembers the name of his Lord and prays, shall indeed be successful.

87.16 But you prefer the life of this world, 87.17. although the Hereafter is better and more lasting. 87.18. This indeed is what is taught in the former scriptures-

The Overwhelming Event (Al-Ghashiyah)

88.1 Have you heard about the Overwhelming Event?

88.8. Some faces on that Day will be radiant, 88.9. well pleased with the result *Of* their striving, 88.10. in a sublime garden, 88.11. where they will hear no idle talk, 88.12. with a flowing spring,88.13. raised couches, 88.14. and goblets set at hand, 88.15. cushions ranged, 88.16. and carpets spread out.

88.21. So, [O Prophet] exhort them: your task is only to exhort, 88.22. you are not their keeper.

88.25. Certainly, it is to Us that they will return. 88.26. Then, surely, it is for Us To call them to account.

The Dawn (Al-Fajr)

89.29. [But to the righteous, God will say], 'O soul at peace, 89.28. return to your Lord, well-pleased, well-pleasing. 89.29. Join My servants. 89.30. Enter My Paradise.'

The City (Al-Balad)

90.4. that We have created man into a life of toil and trial. 90.5. Does he think then that no one has power over him?

The Sun (Al-Shams)

Night (Al-Layl)

92.4.O men, you truly strive towards the most diverse ends! 92.5. As for one who gives [to others] and fears [God], 92.6. and believes in the truth of what is right, 92.7. We will pave his way to ease.

92.12. Surely, it is for Us to provide guidance—88.13. and to Us belongs the Hereafter as well as the present world.

92.17. One who fears God shall be kept away from it—92.18. one who gives his wealth to become purified, 92.19. and owes no favour to anyone, which is to be repaid, 92.20. acting only for the sake of his Lord the Most High— 92.21. and before long he will be well satisfied.

The Glorious Morning Light (Al-Duha)

93.1. By the glorious morning light;93.2. and by the night when it darkens, 93.3. your Lord has not forsaken you, nor is He displeased with you, 93.4. and the Hereafter will indeed be better for you than the present life;93.5. soon you will be gratified with what your Lord will give you. 93.6. Did He not find you orphaned and shelter you? 93.7. Did

He not find you wandering, and give you guidance? 93.8. Did He not find you in want, and make you free from want? 93.9. Therefore do not treat the orphan with harshness, 93.10. and do not chide the one who asks for help; 93.11. but proclaim the blessings of your Lord.

Comfort (Al-Sharh)

94.1. Have We not lifted up your heart, 94.2. and removed your burden 94.3. that weighed so heavily on your back, and 94.4. have We not given

you high renown? 94.5. So, surely with every hardship there is ease; 94.6. surely, with every hardship there is ease. 94.7. So, when you are free, strive hard, 94.8. and to your Lord turn [all] your attention.

The Fig (Al-Tin)

95.4. We have indeed created man in the best of mould,

95.6. except for those who believe and do good deeds—theirs shall be an unending reward!

95.7 What then after this, can make you deny the Last Judgement? 8 Is not God the greatest of the judges?

The Clot (Al-'Alaq)

96.1. Read! In the name of your Lord, who created: 96.2. created man from a clot [of blood]. 96.3. Read! Your Lord is the Most Bountiful One 96.4. who taught by the pen,96.5 taught man what he did not know

96.14. Does he not know that God observes all things?

96.19....but prostrate yourself and come closer to God.

The Night of Destiny (Al-Qadr)

97.1. We sent it [Quran] down on the Night of Destiny. 97.2. And what will make you comprehend what the Night of Destiny is? 97.3. The Night of Destiny is better than a thousand months; 97.4. on that night, the angels and the Spirit come down by the permission of their Lord with His decrees for all matters; 97.5. it is all peace till the break of dawn.

The Clear Evidence (Al-Bayyinah)

98.5. They were commanded only to worship God, offering Him sincere devotion, to be sincere in their faith, to pray regularly; and to give alms, for that is the right religion.

98.7. Truly, those who believe and do good works are the best of creatures. 98.8. God has a reward in store for them: Gardens of eternity, through which rivers flow; they will dwell therein forever. God is well pleased with them and they are well pleased with Him. Thus shall the God-fearing be rewarded.

The Earthquake (Al-Zalzalah)

99.1. When the earth is shaken with its violent shaking, 99.2. when the

earth shakes off her burdens, 99.3. when man asks, 'What is happening to her?'; 99.4. on that Day it will narrate its account,99.5 for your Lord has so directed it. 99.6. On that Day people will come forward in separate groups to be shown their deeds: 99.7. whoever has done the smallest particle of good will see it; 99.8. while whoever has done the smallest particle of evil will see it.

The Snorting Horses (Al-'Adiyat)

100.11. Surely, on that Day, they will know that their Lord had full knowledge of them all.

The Clatterer (Al-Qari'Ah)

Greed for More and More (Al-Takathur)

102.1. Greed for more and more distracted you [from God] 102.2. till you reached the grave. 102.3. But you will soon come to know.

The Passage of Time (Al-'Asr)

103.1. I swear by the passage of time, 103.2. that man is surely in a state of loss, 103.3. except for those who believe and do good deeds and exhort one another to hold fast to the Truth, and who exhort one another to steadfastness.

The Backbiter (Al-Humazah)

The Elephant (Al-Fil)

Quraysh (Quraysh)

Small Things (Al-Ma'Un)

Abundance (Al-Kawthar)

108.1. We have given you abundance. 108.2. Pray to your Lord and sacrifice to Him alone. 108.3. It is the one who hates you who has been cut off.

Those Who Deny the Truth (Al-Kafirun)

109.1. Say, 'You who deny the Truth, 109.2. I do not worship what you worship. 109.3. You do not worship what I worship. 109.4. I will never worship what you worship. 109.5. You will never worship what I worship. 109.6. You have your religion and I have mine.'

Help (Al-Nasr)

110.1. When God's help and victory come, 110.2. and you see people entering God's religion in multitudes, 110.3. then glorify your Lord with His praise and seek His forgiveness. He is always ready to accept repentance.

Twisted Fibre (Al-Masad)
Oneness (Al-Ikhlas)

112.1. Say, 'He is God, the One, 112.2. God, the Self-sufficient One. 112.3. He does not give birth, nor was He born, 112.4. and there is nothing like Him.'

Daybreak (Al-Falaq)

113.1. Say, 'I seek refuge in the Lord of the daybreak 113.2. from the evil of what He has created, 113.3. from the evil of darkness as it descends, 113.4. from the evil of those who blow on knots 113.5. and from the evil of the envier when he envies.'

People (Al-Nas)

114.1. Say, 'I seek refuge in the Lord of people, 114.2. the King of people, 114.3. the God of people, 114.4. from the mischief of every sneaking whisperer, 114.5. who whispers into the hearts of people, 114.6. from jinn and men.'

EPILOGUE

God is the light of the heavens and the earth.

In this universe the human being is a special creation who has been given the exceptional powers of hearing, seeing, thinking and decision making. These capacities have been given to human for a special purpose, namely, to understand the reality of life. S/he should use ears to hear the voice of Truth. Use eyes to see the signs of God that are spread all around. S/he should use thinking powers for an in-depth study of all these things and decide accordingly. This, in reality, is the way of thankfulness of the ears, the eyes and the inner self. Those who give evidence of such thankfulness in this world have the entitlement to these gifts forever.

Holy Quran is the word of **GOD** who is the **ALMIGHTY**, who is the **CREATOR**, who is the SUSTAINER, who is the GUIDE. 59.22. He is God: there is no deity save Him. He knows the unseen and the visible. He is the Compassionate, the Merciful. 59.23. He is God, there is no deity save Him, the Sovereign, the Most Pure, the Source of Peace, the Granter of Security, the Protector, the Mighty, the Subduer, the Supreme, Glory be to God, who is far above what they associate with Him. 59.24. He is God—the Creator, the Originator, the Giver of Form. His are the most excellent names. Everything in the heavens and earth declares His glory. He is the Mighty, the Wise One.

It is a message of hope from HIM to humankind.

Let us believe in HIM.

Let us be positive thinkers.

Let us study Quran.

Let us hope.

THANK YOU

Don't miss out!

Visit the website below and you can sign up to receive emails whenever yusuf jamal publishes a new book. There's no charge and no obligation.

https://books2read.com/r/B-A-DIFZ-IQALC

BOOKS2READ

Connecting independent readers to independent writers.

About the Author

Professor Yusuf Jamal is a renowned teacher and research scholar in Physiology currently working at Delhi University, New Delhi, India.. He has published many books on medical as well as non medical subjects. Spiritual development of his students is also his passion. Taherefore this book is presented to all of you.

Read more at physiology4u.blogspot.com.